MANAGEMENT SKILL GUIDE

MANAGING PERFORMANCE APPRAISAL

Lesley Myland

Croner Publications Limited
Croner House
London Road
Kingston upon Thames
Surrey KT2 6SR
Telephone: 081-547 3333

First published 1992
Reprinted 1992

Published by
Croner Publications Ltd,
Croner House,
London Road,
Kingston upon Thames,
Surrey KT2 6SR
Telephone: 081-547 3333

Typeset by Avonset, Midsomer Norton, Bath
Printed and bound in Great Britain by
Biddles Ltd, Guildford and King's Lynn

Contents

Introduction   1

Part 1 — The Background to Performance Appraisal   5

Chapter 1   Introduction   7
Chapter 2   The Meaning of Performance Appraisal   9
Chapter 3   Considering Relevant Objectives for Performance Appraisal   17
Chapter 4   Overcoming the Problems of Performance Appraisal   27
Chapter 5   Conclusion   33

Part 2 — Introducing or Revising a Performance Appraisal Scheme   37

Chapter 1   Introduction   39
Chapter 2   Creating the Right Climate   41
Chapter 3   Getting Started — Consulting Users   43
Chapter 4   Formulating Objectives   45
Chapter 5   Designing a Performance Appraisal Scheme — the Options   47
Chapter 6   Procedural Aspects   65
Chapter 7   Communication and Training   69
Chapter 8   Conclusion   75

Part 3 — Carrying Out Performance Appraisal Effectively   81

Chapter 1   Introduction   83
Chapter 2   Writing or Revising Job Descriptions   85
Chapter 3   Preparing for the Appraisal Meeting   93
Chapter 4   Conducting Appraisal Interviews   103
Chapter 5   Agreeing Action Plans   115
Chapter 6   Following Up   121
Chapter 7   Conclusion   125

Check-list for Managing Performance Appraisal   131

Index   133

Introduction

Today's working climate demands a great deal of commitment and effort from employees, who in their turn naturally expect a great deal more from their employers. The development of a much more participative style of management in many organisations is a positive step towards meeting such heightened expectations. This participative style can be expressed in a variety of practical ways, such as team briefings or quality circles, and of course regular performance appraisal. Performance appraisal is designed to maximise effectiveness by bringing participation to a more individual level in that it provides a forum for consultation about standards of work, potential, aspirations and concerns. It is an opportunity for employees to have a significantly greater influence upon the quality of their working lives. In these times of emphasis on "quality", there is a natural equation: better quality goods and services come from employees who enjoy better quality "goods and services" from their employers.

Looking ahead to the typical employee of the next decade or so, it is worth considering that the current National Curriculum places emphasis on continuous assessment and appraisal. It therefore follows that most employers are now having to embrace a generation who would expect to be aware of their goals, how to achieve them, how they are matching up to them, and what to do if they are not. In short, they would expect some sort of performance appraisal to be a normal part of their employment contract.

In introducing or revising a performance appraisal scheme, it should be said that there is not one "right" way to do it. The most appropriate route to take will depend upon the current style and status of the organisation. It would seem, however, that there are a number of "wrong" ways! Certain aspects of the history and development of performance appraisal have almost certainly led to some negative attitudes about it. There are common complaints such as: "It's just a yearly rollicking", or "It's like school report time", or "Nothing comes out of it anyway". Clearly, a significant consideration in choosing how to go about introducing or revising a scheme will be an understanding of how such attitudes have been perpetuated and how they might be overcome. People carry bad experiences with them for a long time, in this case, perhaps from job to job. Much has to be done at the time of introducing or revising a performance appraisal scheme to reassure those who will be involved that intentions are sincere and positive.

Performance appraisal must be seen as an intrinsic part of a manager's responsibilities, not an unwelcome and time-consuming addition to them. It is about improving performance and ultimately effectiveness — all part of the manager's basic remit. Bearing this in mind, it is inappropriate to see performance appraisal as the property of the personnel department. Although personnel has a most significant role to play, namely in terms of expert advice, administration and review, it would be unfortunate if managers came to see appraisal as another form-filling exercise from a support department, and that any action required as a result of it could be safely deposited along with the returned report. The message is that it is the responsibility of line managers to carry out and follow up performance appraisal with their own staff, using whatever resources are available to make it effective.

This book is designed for managers and personnel specialists who have to make performance appraisal work in their organisations. This may be at a senior level looking into the whole issue of introduction or revision. Equally, it can be for those who feel the need to know more so that they can be better appraisers. It will also be useful for those involved in consultation groups whose brief is to make recommendations about introducing performance appraisal into their organisations.

The following pages should answer many questions. They will probably pose as many more and the answers to these questions will only be found "on the ground", where performance appraisal is to be used. Whatever points are raised, whatever options are explored, the ultimate decision in how to manage performance appraisal in an organisation will rest with those who "own" the scheme — the appraisers and the appraisees.

Finally, a note on the structure of the book is appropriate. It is divided into three parts, each dealing with quite different aspects of managing performance appraisal.

Part 1 deals with background issues: the meaning of appraisal, its purpose in the context of managing people and overcoming potential problems.

Part 2 provides an insight into the many considerations of introducing or revising a performance appraisal scheme: creating the right climate, formulating objectives, scheme design and communication.

Part 3 deals with the practical elements of appraising people: preparing, interviewing and following up.

The intention is to provide a pathway through the options in establishing a system of monitoring and improving the performance and commitment of any organisation's most valuable resource — its employees. Appraisal can be dangerous in uncommitted, unenlightened and untrained hands, but approached with due care and attention, it can be a manager's most useful ally.

Part 1

The Background to Performance Appraisal

Chapter 1
Introduction

On the matter of considering the relevance of performance appraisal to an organisation, the first question which should be asked at senior levels is: "What are we seeking to introduce into the organisation and why?".

Any self-respecting, would-be appraiser, might also ask: "Why should I be doing this?". The question can be further defined: "What is it anyway? What is the point of it all? Why does the organisation want me to spend all this time and effort on it?".

Perhaps, at junior levels, a rather more introspective sort of curiosity may be aroused: "What is this appraisal thing anyway? What is in it for me?".

To answer these questions, Part 1 deals with what performance appraisal really is and its place in the wider context of managing people.

Chapter 2
The Meaning of Performance Appraisal

A simple definition of performance appraisal is that it is a systematic means of ensuring that managers and their staff meet regularly to discuss past and present performance issues, and to agree what future action is appropriate on both sides.

This meeting should be based on a clear and mutual understanding of the job in question, and the standards and outcomes which are a part of it. In normal circumstances, employees would be appraised by their immediate managers on a one-to-one basis.

In considering what performance appraisal is, it is worthwhile adding a note about what it is *not*. One or two traditional methods in carrying out appraisal have led to some misconceptions about it. Often, the distinction between assessing performance and appraising it is not made. Assessment concerns itself only with the past and present. Staff are being appraised when they are encouraged to look ahead to improve effectiveness, utilise strengths, redress weaknesses, and examine how potential and aspirations match up.

It should also be understood that pushing a previously prepared report across a desk, cursorily inviting comment, and expecting it to be meekly signed by the employee is not appraisal — this is merely a form-filling exercise which achieves little in terms of giving staff any positive guidance and motivation.

Regular, performance, agree and *future* are some of the key words in the definition offered in the first paragraph and a closer look at what these words imply is necessary to gain an understanding of the term "performance appraisal".

Regularity

Regular performance appraisal would be defined as once or twice a year in most organisations. Some managers may say that since they appraise their people on an ongoing basis throughout the year such a ritualistic routine is quite unnecessary. This approach is not an unworthy one, since assessment of performance can only be valid if it is a continuous process and issues are dealt with as they arise. However, the point of having a landmark in the procedure is so that the period under review can be formally summed up and this summary seen as the starting point for the next review period. A good proportion of managers would agree that this sort of discipline makes them much more conscientious as appraisers. An even larger proportion would probably admit that they would not appraise at all without such a discipline.

The appraisee's viewpoint should not be overlooked in this matter. Some employees are most willing to communicate about everything and anything at any time, and the idea of continuous dialogue about their performance is very acceptable to them. Others find communicating a problem at the best of times and the occasion of a thoughtfully conducted appraisal interview will help them to overcome this difficulty.

There is some danger that the appraisal may become "paper based", in that completing a six monthly or yearly report form becomes the focus of the exercise. This can be avoided by making managers aware of exactly what outcomes are required by the appraisal process, and those would rarely include extra paperwork for its own sake. A more likely requirement would be evidence that thorough discussion has taken place and that a relevant plan of action is being undertaken as a result.

Whatever the manager's approach to regularity in appraising staff, the rule "no surprises" must be absolutely sacrosanct (no points saved up and no punches pulled). It might be unrealistic to insist that staff comply with this rule, but the process of ongoing appraisal should encourage them to understand the benefits of voicing their concerns as they occur.

Performance

Results and Behaviour

Performance in a job is a matter which needs to be considered both in terms of results achieved and behaviour demonstrated.

Results required in relation to quantity, quality or timing can be established in most aspects of a large number of jobs. Comparing results reached to results required is essential in evaluating performance. However, this is not always a straightforward matter. It would not be appropriate to applaud success when every rule in the book has been broken in achieving it! Neither would it be correct to denigrate totally a shortfall in requirements when sincere attempts to reach the standard are evident. Therefore, reviewing results in the context of actions and behaviour is necessary to develop a full understanding of individual performance. In determining what actions have lead to success or the lack of it, this aspect of examining performance will represent a significant element in forming plans for the future, so that strengths can be built upon and weaknesses addressed.

There are, of course, certain jobs or features of certain jobs, where it is not always possible to state a required result or standard that clearly. In these instances considering behaviour assumes a greater significance when appraising performance. The manager of a home for the elderly, for example, would be able to show ability in controlling budgets in a tangible manner by keeping within certain financial guidelines. The most important part of such a job however, would concern the health and well-being of residents. Apart from being difficult to measure, these aspects could be somewhat beyond the manager's control, and it would be unfair to make an assessment on the amount of medicines used or the mortality rate. Therefore it follows that the manager's actions in promoting the good health and well-being of residents are the most relevant factor in evaluating performance, rather than results. In this case, examples of such action might be ensuring that specialised help is summoned when necessary, listening to residents who want to talk about their problems, or perhaps arranging appropriate diversions and entertainment.

What not to Appraise

Disciplinary Issues

The inclusion of disciplinary matters in appraisal by some organisations almost certainly contributes to some negative attitudes about the process.

Strictly speaking, in carrying out *performance* appraisal, items which belong in the disciplinary arena such as time-keeping or appearance are not up for discussion. Problems relating to these points of conduct would normally be dealt with as and when they arose, and persistent offenders would ultimately go through the prescribed sequence of disciplinary warnings. The stage at which points of conduct might be discussed in appraisal is when they affect performance, for example, sales people not making sales because they always turn up late for appointments. In this instance the issue is being addressed as an element of behaviour resulting in low achievement, rather than as a matter of discipline. It would be necessary, however, to make this distinction clear to the appraisee and refer to the fact that the matter has been, or might well be, discussed as a disciplinary issue at some point.

One of the benefits of continuous appraisal, is that performance problems can be nipped in the bud, but if they do reach the disciplinary stage it may be better to postpone an appraisal meeting, if one is due, until a more positive climate is established. (This decision would need to be formally agreed and recorded with the individual lest it be construed as unfair treatment.) If the appraisal were to go ahead, it would be essential to indicate what matters are under review in the disciplinary procedure in a written summary and record that the meeting had considered the more positive aspects of performance. The appraisal should never ignore problems and employees must not be confused about where they stand. However, entering into another discussion during the appraisal could well turn it into an additional showdown. Apart from being undesirable this would also be unconstitutional, for when a disciplinary meeting is to be held employees are entitled to reasonable warning that this is the case. The ACAS code of practice also recommends that employees should be allowed to bring along a representative.

To drift into a disciplinary forum would deny these rights and could be deemed to be unfair.

Personality

Appraising performance should be held to mean literally that, and not appraising personality and personal characteristics. The subjectivity of such an approach makes it impossible for it to be particularly meaningful, and it is also difficult to produce an action plan for the future based on restructuring personality! Additionally this approach is too personal and emotive to be well received by appraisers or appraisees. The prospect of having to criticise people's nature openly is not a welcoming one for most managers. It is even less pleasant to be on the receiving end of such criticism.

Many managers would argue that particular characteristics are essential for certain jobs and must therefore be appraised. The matter of how correct assumptions are about what characteristics really are necessary to do certain jobs is too complex to go into here, but given the belief that the salesperson must be an extrovert, or the social worker must be sympathetic, what is to be done if there is some evidence that a lack of these qualities is affecting results? The matter needs to be discussed in clear behavioural terms, not as an issue of personality. Only then will the assessment have any validity or acceptability, and only then can some relevant action plans be agreed to overcome the problem.

This point is illustrated by the example of the secretary who was described by her boss as lacking in confidence and initiative. What led him to make these judgments was the fact that she seemed unwilling or unable to organise his diary without constantly asking him what she should arrange for when. Her job description stated quite clearly that she was responsible for making all diary arrangements for her manager and that she was required only to communicate them to him at appropriate intervals. Naturally, the shortfall in performance in this area of her job seemed like a lack of confidence and initiative. The matter was discussed in this light, and feeling unable to do much about her personal short-comings the secretary did not improve matters. Fortunately, a third party suggested to the manager that he should try talking about the problem from a more constructive standpoint: "Ask her why she wants you to sanction everything and when you have discussed the reasons, work out a suitable plan to enable her to organise your diary the way you want it done." The manager revised his approach and discovered that his own rather haphazard organisation was partly to blame for the problem. Between them, the manager and his secretary worked out a system, including more regular meetings, to enable them to get the diary system working well.

Agreement

Performance appraisal should be seen by those involved as an opportunity for honest discussion. In this discussion, the appraiser does not judge but promotes agreement about how current performance matches up to requirements and how the future might be approached. The record of the appraisal interview should in fact be an agreed summary of the discussion, from which a description of current performance and future action plans must be discernible. Making it clear that this is what is meant by performance appraisal, will go some way towards removing apprehension about it. Appraisers do not have to contemplate a scene where they are obliged either to patronise, criticise or confront someone with whom they wish to continue a relatively trouble-free working relationship. Appraisees do not have to imagine the prospect of emerging from an appraisal interview labelled, for example, as "This person is only average".

Future

Considering the future in performance appraisal can be a matter of aiming towards improving performance in the existing job to bring it up to minimum required standards. It can also be about developing a good performer with the object of enhancing job satisfaction and ensuring that maximum potential is being reached both by the job holder and by the job itself. Additionally, it can be about assisting individuals to progress towards different or more responsible positions within the organisation or profession.

When looking to the future in performance appraisal, a great deal of objectivity and realism must be applied. Is the organisation in a position to offer much anyway? Resources and opportunities may be scarce, however temporarily. False promises must not be made, although it may tempting to do this rather than disappoint a keen employee.

The term "future" will have different relevance in different circumstances. For example, there are certain individuals who do a perfectly good job and the future to them is a desire to be left alone, within reason, to carry on doing so. There is little wrong with providing the recognition which is due in such a case, acknowledging the *status quo*, and proceeding accordingly.

Another possibility might be the necessity to deal with those who have burning ambitions and who, at least for the time being, do not have the ability to realise them. Facing facts as they stand is important, but so is a positive approach towards assisting the individual to develop in the right direction. At the very worst, trying and failing will demonstrate just how much needs to be done before promotion can be realistically planned.

When communicating the intentions of appraisal to potential appraisers and appraisees alike it is necessary to emphasise that "future" does not necessarily imply promotion or development. It may simply mean planning towards a better performance in the existing job. For some, it may mean acknowledgement that the job is being done well and encouragement to carry on doing so.

Summing Up

In order to derive the maximum benefit from performance appraisal it must be viewed in the most positive light by potential users. Therefore, it is important, that the definition offered in this chapter is carefully considered, and that any possibility of the event becoming a pseudo-disciplinary arena, a character assassination attempt, or a place where promises are made and not kept, is reduced to the minimum.

Chapter 3
Considering Relevant Objectives for Performance Appraisal

A major step in devising a performance appraisal scheme is deciding exactly why it is desirable to have one. What outcomes are required from the amount of effort which must go into such a project? What return is required from the investment? Organisations need to consider their objectives long before they design their schemes, if they are to ensure progress towards meeting these objectives.

To establish the relevance of objectives in performance appraisal they have to be considered in the light of organisational objectives. Is there a statement of plans for the next three to five years? Are the objectives of the appraisal scheme consistent with those plans? Objectives must also be considered in the much wider context of people management and how they relate to organisational priorities in maximising human resources.

Appraisal and Management Style

The practice of monitoring and improving performance is all part of being a good manager. Consulting on problems, nipping concerns in the bud, maintaining standards, assisting in reaching targets and improving effectiveness are some of the ways in which results are obtained through people. A regular stock-take and a look ahead would be entirely consistent with such a management style and a performance appraisal scheme fits in well with managing people in this way.

What is self-evident, however, is that introducing performance appraisal into an organisation whose management style is generally autocratic would be something of an anomaly. It would also be doomed to failure, since it would be greeted with a fair degree of suspicion ("What on earth are they up to now?"). Commitment to it would be lacking.

There have been some good examples of organisations which have seen the introduction or revision of an appraisal scheme as a natural extension to their increasing professionalism in a participative style of management. There have been as many examples of organisations who have felt unrest about management growing in the workforce and have introduced an appraisal scheme as an attempt to do something about it. All that this approach would achieve would be to make matters worse. If unrest is manifesting itself, the whole management approach may need to be rationalised. To expect an appraisal scheme to sort everything out is unrealistic. It is unlikely that there would be the infrastructure to handle the feedback resulting from the appraisal round and this would increase problems. In this event, suspicions would be vindicated and the credibility of the organisation's management seriously damaged.

A stated objective of a performance appraisal scheme could well be something like:

> To assist staff in performing their job to the best of their ability, thus maximising their job satisfaction and their contribution to the company's objectives.

This is a legitimate and worthwhile objective, but would only have meaning in an organisation where it reflects the way in which employees are normally managed.

Appraisal and Communication

Since appraisal is a particularly refined form of corporate communication, using it to improve communications is a relevant objective. This applies both to communication on a one-to-one basis between managers and staff, and to management communication in general. Here is an opportunity to ensure that all issues relating to performance are clarified and to exchange information in order to improve operational effectiveness.

Seen as a way of strengthening good communications, performance appraisal has a rightful place in an organisation's communications policy. What must be avoided, however, is introducing appraisal because communications are bad. This is rather like the unhappily married couple who thought that starting a family would solve their problems but found that their worries were compounded by the additional responsibilities. An appraisal scheme will not create better corporate communication on its own. It can only serve as part of a system where regular updates, team briefings, meetings and consultation are the norm. As with management style, problems can be made worse by introducing a system out of step with the general climate. If communication is bad, what is going to happen to all the feedback obtained from appraisees? There is a strong likelihood that it will fade away under the pressures of day-to-day operational needs, never to be heard of again until a disillusioned member of staff asks "Whatever did happen to ...?".

Appraisal and Motivation

It is impossible to generalise about motivation when discussing human nature and every individual must be seen as just that — an individual. However, in broad terms, it is now understood that achievement, recognition, involvement, job satisfaction and development are more likely to motivate than anything else, given that they are provided in satisfactory working conditions and that rewards are appropriate.

Appraisal links into the motivational aspect of the manager's job in that it can be aimed at giving recognition, helping people achieve, involving them, assisting in creating job satisfaction and providing a forum in which to discuss development. There is a saying that "People leave bosses, not jobs". How individuals are managed has a direct relevance to how motivated they are likely to be. There is no doubt that appraisal, well handled, strengthens relationships because of the opportunities it creates for good quality communication.

Appraisal also offers a good opportunity for managers to keep in touch with their employees' changing capabilities and aspirations. Individuals do not stay the same for very long, although it is often convenient to believe that they do. The human condition is always to go on wanting, and self-realisation is a temporary state for most individuals. People "grow" and are capable of taking on more as time passes, or circumstances change freeing them to offer more.

This principle can apply just as much in reverse. Managers may find that some members of staff have had all the status and responsibility they can handle. For these people, helping them achieve satisfaction in their working lives is more likely to be a matter of making adjustments to accommodate reduced capacity. In such cases, the important issue is that honest communication has taken place and that such adjustments are seen as a benefit for those concerned, not a loss of face.

Performance appraisal also complements the idea that with agreed levels of attainment individuals will work willingly and reasonably independently towards achieving goals. Under such circumstances only support and guidance is needed from the manager, not constant instruction and checking. A manager, in demonstrating the belief that employees can achieve, is going a long way to ensuring that they will.

For managers who take the motivation of their staff seriously, performance appraisal is an indispensable tool. The "added value" is the satisfaction managers themselves derive from appraising staff well and seeing the results it can bring in terms of increased ability, commitment and achievement.

Appraisal and Reward

Money

There is something fundamentally right about allowing those who achieve more and contribute more in an organisation to reap a larger proportion of the rewards it has to offer.

As a basis for distributing pay, a performance appraisal scheme can be helpful, particularly if it concentrates on quantifiable standards and targets. It is certainly better than some alternatives, which may amount to no more than a series of subjective decisions about who "deserves" what.

However, the disadvantages of linking reward to appraisal may outweigh the advantages. The problem of relating pay and performance is that, for it to be absolutely fair, everyone must be *enabled* consistently. The abilities of employees' immediate superiors, both as managers and assessors, is rarely uniformly good across an organisation. Similarly, the distribution of resources is often inconsistent, resulting in difficulties which may mean that the potential for good performance is frustrated. Often performance is affected by other matters beyond the control of managers or subordinates.

An additional problem is demonstrated by the experience of a large public service which had to abandon its performance-related pay scheme due to pressure from employees who found that it put too much emphasis on quantity rather than quality and that standards had ceased to be important.

Another public service allocates a certain amount of money each year for pay increases to those staff who have reached objectives. In any one year, if the majority of staff reach their objectives there is not enough money to give meaningful increases to those who have earned them. The trade union representing the staff of this institution has lodged an official objection to the continuation of this policy, which it has deemed to be unrealistic and demotivating.

One certain fact about linking reward to appraisal is that people are unlikely to shoot themselves in the foot. If an objective of appraisal is to provide a basis for distributing pay awards, the objective of improving communication may be negated. Making waves, asking for help, admitting to needing training or agreeing about a shortfall in results, will not come readily to appraisees who know that they need to be perceived as performing well to get a better pay award. People may not work primarily for money, but its fair distribution has an amazing significance. Pride, dignity and recognition are some of the other complexities involved in this particular issue.

All this having been said, it is better to have some form of assessment upon which to base pay awards than none at all. Otherwise, all that may be left is an arbitrary system which cannot be scrupulously fair. If reward and appraisal must be linked, one way of minimising difficulties might be to separate the appraisal and the pay review on the calendar.

A large retail organisation organised its appraisal round in April and May each year, and its pay award in October. The two exercises were not, in theory, linked at the time of the actual appraisal interview, although staff were well aware that their appraisals would be looked at for the purpose of distributing pay awards six months later. The central issue at award time, however, was not the picture of employees which had emerged at the appraisal. More important was how they had performed since in achieving targets and addressing problems. The system was well received by employees and seemed to work, although no doubt a careful study of it would reveal that even this "ideal" approach was as imperfect as anything which operates in such a potentially emotive area.

It seems hardly necessary to add that to decide the amount of a pay award before the appraisal interview and to deliver it during the process is inappropriate. This would strengthen any suspicions that the employees' input to the discussion was superfluous and be a cause for anxiety of both appraiser and appraisee.

A pessimistic point about linking appraisal and pay is that in hard times there may be no money to distribute. Will appraisal have to stop when the going gets tough (when it is probably needed most)? Shifting the emphasis from pay to mere verbal recognition would be enough to destroy management credibility at a stroke.

There is no right answer to the question "Shall we relate appraisal and pay?". If an organisation wants to do so, then it must look into all the pros and cons. The decision is made knowing what the benefits are likely to be and, just as importantly, what the possible drawbacks are.

Promotion

The concept of discussing promotion potential and career planning has been questioned from time to time. For certain employees the exercise may have little point if such issues are not discussed. However, a prime contender for an impending promotional opportunity is not necessarily going to be completely honest about current problem areas at an appraisal interview.

A similar observation applies in this matter as in that of relating pay to appraisal, most notably that some searching discussion may be prevented by the possibility of raising doubts about potential. Career planning is too important both to individuals and to organisations to tuck it in as part of another exercise. To give it due emphasis, and to remove a possible obstacle to the appraisal process, career planning may well need to be the subject of a separate exercise.

Every organisation has to find the formula which is right for it. Meanwhile, if career prospects are brought up at appraisal time, as they almost inevitably will be, appraisers must feel no pressure to discuss promotion in anything but a completely honest and realistic light. Is the opportunity there? Is this person capable of taking it at the moment? Could plans be laid for future development?

An Employment Benefit

A company in south-east England advertised "staff appraisal" alongside items such as health schemes, subsidised lunches and season ticket loans, as an employment benefit. It also placed "good communications" on the list. The less cynical saw this as a novel idea — to place appraisal alongside the more usual "perks". The more cynical saw it as a way of indicating that a scheme of performance-related pay was operated. The organisation concerned would not commit itself either way when asked, but the concept seems to be a progressive one. This organisation demonstrated faith enough in appraisal actually to advertise it as a benefit.

Appraisal and Performance Standards

Discussing and agreeing standards of performance is an ongoing part of the manager's job, as is continual assessment and considering how to maximise performance potential. Appraisal is a formal extension of this responsibility, and given that it is carried out with commitment and a degree of skill by managers, raising levels of efficiency in the organisation as a whole is a natural outcome. This would not necessarily have to be a stated objective — most tend quite rightly to focus on the individual. Nevertheless, the point will be made indirectly — to assist employees in performing their jobs to the best of their ability is to maximise their contribution to the organisation's aims.

Appraisal, and Training and Development

To analyse training and development needs is often a stated objective of performance appraisal, and one which focuses both on benefits to the individual and to the organisation.

There is no doubt that this is a valid objective but it must be seen in context. To discover a widespread training need only as a result of appraisal is reactive rather than proactive management. An analysis of training and development requirements can best be achieved by carrying out an exercise devised for that purpose alone. Such an analysis, to be accurate and worthwhile, could be complex and time-consuming. It is an unnecessary added complication to have to extricate the analysis from a mountain of appraisal report forms. That exercise will be carried out at a later stage and will serve to fine-tune and customise departmental and individual needs. Unless training needs are assessed separately, appraisal feedback may result in some distorted reactions not necessarily related to organisational requirements. This situation was demonstrated by the engineering company which found itself with 20 employees who had been promised training for relief reception duty, when the real need was for a team of only four or five.

The real benefit of appraisal in this area, is that it reaffirms that managers are responsible for the training and development of their own staff, albeit with the help of a training specialist. An appraisal report form with the appropriate reminders on it, creates an added discipline to ensure that managers are aware of this responsibility.

A relevant part of appraisal feedback may be the type of training method most suited to individual employees. This would probably be outside the scope of a company-wide analysis, but it is a key factor in determining the success, or otherwise, of any training undertaken by an employee. Some people learn well in a seminar environment, others need plenty of practical experience. Some enjoy theoretical learning, others need to immerse themselves in daily routines in order to learn. Appraiser and appraisee discussing previous training experiences, agreeing the best options and formalising what improvements are expected to result from learning, is the most pertinent way to ensure that any training carried out actually has some impact.

Evaluation of training is also part of the appraisal process, since any plans for training made during an appraisal must be thoroughly followed up. Again, evaluation of training should be carried out as a separate, specifically designed exercise, but the information obtained at an appraisal will be an additional indicator as to how well training resources are being used.

Appraisal and Planning

Planning current and future staffing needs is a legitimate aim in performance appraisal, although not always an easy one to reach coherently, because of the many influences which can frustrate or alter the most comprehensive planning system.

Manpower Planning

Consistently applied across an organisation, performance appraisal should give a wealth of data about who is in the right job, who wants to change jobs and who should be considered for development or promotion.

Job Content

Feedback from job holders often gives a better insight into the evolution which takes place almost imperceptibly in certain jobs.

Appraisal is an ideal situation in which to discuss and recognise changes in job content which have not been previously formalised, although feedback obtained here would have to be handled very objectively.

An individual may have stopped performing a key task of the job description because they do not like it and could have coerced others into doing it for them. This does not alter the fact that they should be doing it, and operational needs determine that they should still at least carry out the function when necessary. Staff might even try to get a particularly unpopular routine dropped because they all insist that it just is not really necessary any more. The possibilities here are endless if the manager is not objective enough to collate feedback and review it in relation to departmental and organisational needs. The main task here is to follow through and either to make appropriate changes or to explain why no changes can be made.

Evaluating Trends

Additionally, appraisal can be extremely useful in highlighting certain trends. On the basis that not all of the people can be wrong all of the time, some issues may emerge which need attention at senior level. Additionally, individual managers can learn a great deal about the impact of their management style and practices, and how they might make changes for the better.

Appraisal and Record Keeping

Whilst appraisal should never be a "paper based" procedure, a record of it is essential for some sensible reasons. For instance, a new manager to a department would need a clear indication of what performance standards might be expected and what ongoing targets are. Some would prefer to make their own decisions and refer to previous appraisals only for confirmation, or the reverse, of their own findings, but they would need at least some point of reference.

An action plan would definitely need to be written down, and it is always practical to have a record of employees' performance standards, aspirations and potential for planning purposes or possibly for the allocation of salary awards.

On a less positive note, an appraisal may well be admissible in evidence if an employee takes a former employer to an industrial tribunal claiming unfair dismissal. This emphasises the need for the appraisal report to be absolutely accurate in what it has to impart about performance, even if this is by cross-reference to disciplinary proceedings.

Appraisal and Staff Retention

The demographic trends which are likely to manifest themselves in the late 1990s will see many organisations competing for a scarce resource — new staff to fill vacancies. Many vacancies are unavoidable through retirement, illness, leaving the area or sheer incompatibility. However, many "casualties" can be avoided if managers can address themselves to some of the other issues which cause staff to leave for alternative employment — frustration, boredom, lack of opportunity, lack of recognition, etc. Both continuous and formal appraisal must be seen as a way of identifying problems before they reach the point of no return and another employee ends up as a statistic on the labour turnover analysis.

The Benefits of Performance Appraisal

Considering the objectives of performance appraisal in the context of managing people is to consider its many benefits. These benefits will apply in varying proportions to organisations, to managers and to individuals. When introducing or revising an appraisal scheme, considering how these benefits can be communicated with confidence and sincerity to all users is an important part of setting out the objectives of the scheme.

When formulating objectives, there is no rule about how many or in what order. The only rule is that they are meaningful, achievable, consistent with organisational aims and do not conflict with each other (eg a relationship with pay may hinder an objective to improve communication).

Chapter 4
Overcoming the Problems of Performance Appraisal

No argument is complete without consideration of all sides. Outlining the objectives of performance appraisal and attendant benefits is an indispensable exercise if there are parties to be persuaded that the idea is worthwhile. Showing that the downside of the argument has also been evaluated will demonstrate a much more comprehensive approach to the matter and will therefore produce a more convincing case.

Most problems associated with performance appraisal are not related to the principal of having a scheme so much as to how it is implemented. Therefore, these points need to be discussed in the chapters dealing with the elements of carrying out appraisal. However, there are some broader concerns which need to be thought out before performance appraisal can be introduced.

Time

Appraising properly takes a great deal of time and effort which is not always easy to make room for in today's results-orientated commercial climate. There really can be no compromise in this matter — appraisal has to be accepted as a time-consuming exercise. This time should be seen as an investment, but such a concept is not always an easy one to grasp, for the returns are frequently very long term. It must be clear from the outset that an appraisal scheme may not reap obvious major benefits for perhaps a couple of years.

Ability

Any appraisal scheme is vulnerable to various kinds of misuse. Regardless of what particular system is used (and each of these brings its own problems as will be discussed in the "options" chapter), there will be variations in how well managers carry out appraisal. No matter how competently training is carried out or how well the scheme is monitored at senior levels, there will always be participants who think they know better, who have no commitment to the process, or who are simply incapable. This particular problem serves to emphasise not only how important communication and training are, but also how vital it is for senior managers to monitor the scheme conscientiously.

Paperwork and Job Descriptions

Some organisations have a cultural resistance to the more practical elements of appraisal, such as completing forms. Care must be taken to design "user friendly" paperwork which does not impose an unnecessary and irrelevant burden on appraisers.

An even greater resistance may be voiced to the idea of describing jobs and many people fall at this hurdle in the process of implementing an appraisal scheme. It is often felt to be too restrictive a practice in an organisation where flexibility is the key to getting things done. This is a more common problem in small organisations, although some larger ones still feel that describing jobs equals demarcation. The truth is that if employees become inflexible because they have job descriptions, the problem is way beyond the fact that job descriptions are being used. A long hard look at how staff are managed and motivated is required.

It remains that if performance is to be appraised, then exactly what the elements of that performance are must be clear to appraisers and appraisees. Additionally, some measurable standards must be apparent so that there can be an objective assessment of what has been achieved. Failing to provide some solid and objective basis upon which to carry out the appraisal process may well result in it becoming an extremely subjective exercise. Worse still, it may lean towards appraising personality and very general aspects of behaviour because there is no structure to prevent it from doing so. This leads to vague outcomes, since no action plans can be formulated based upon definite result areas. All this adds up to the possibility of an appraisal scheme with little credibility.

All this taken into account, some organisations do have valid reasons for not wishing to impose job descriptions, whilst still wishing to have some form of appraisal scheme. These organisations have a long history of good, productive staff relations which they have no wish to disrupt. This may not be the right approach for the future of the organisation when it will need to recruit from a generation with quite different expectations. However, long-term prospects may appear to have no relevance to current working patterns in cases like this, and putting off more formal employment practices is quite understandable. What must be clear in this situation is that the burden of keeping the appraisal objective and productive is considerably heavier. It can be done, but a great deal of personal effort and discipline will be required on the part of appraisers.

Attitudes

The prevalence of negative attitudes, however they may have been formed, can seem to be too deeply rooted ever to be effectively eradicated. Only a long-term commitment, demonstrated by tangible actions designed to prove the worth of an appraisal scheme, will make any difference to the idea that appraisal is merely an annual ritual or rebuke. Change for the better, however minimal, must be a perceptible outcome of appraisal right from the very beginning. A lack of reaction in the early stages will often see commitment fade and the attempt to change attitudes fail, because of disillusionment and frustration.

Structure

Some organisations will feel that their operating structure does not lend itself to the idea of "one person one boss" meeting on a regular basis.

The problem of a workforce scattered over widespread locations, makes any form of communication difficult and the logistics of interviewing everyone on a regular basis are almost impossible. The answer to such a practical problem may be to get appraisees to travel to their manager, although this does not address the issue of how meaningful the appraisal would be if ongoing dialogue throughout the year has been restricted by locational difficulties. There is a potential to argue that if this is the case, these people are not being managed well anyway, but often resources determine that no other alternatives exist. The argument must be counterbalanced by the point that appraisal is even more important in such a remote management situation. One topic for discussion at such an appraisal is how all parties can make their situation work best. Appraisal is not designed to disrupt the *status quo* if it is working as well as it can. It will have to operate within given constraints and make the most of them.

There are often problems of sheer team size. To manage 30 people effectively is difficult enough, but to appraise them all fairly is nearly impossible. One answer may be to subdivide the team into smaller sections and train team leaders in all aspects of people management, not just how to appraise. This of course may not be possible or desirable and does go against the trend towards "flatter" management structures.

The employee who has several bosses of equal status, may present a problem. An example of this relationship would be the secretary to a team of sales managers. Who appraises in such a case? Perhaps the answer is for the sales managers' manager to be responsible for the secretary. Appraisal, after all, is not the only matter at issue here. A variety of problems may arise in the course of any individual's employment — it is necessary to know where to go to get them sorted out. Another answer is for someone in this sort of situation to report to a senior secretary who will manage the individual in consultation with those for whom secretarial services are provided. Whatever the solution decided upon, something must be done. Four sales managers getting together for a constructive appraisal discussion with their secretary seems an unlikely scenario.

Project workers who might work for several different project managers during one review period must retain links with one manager who is to be regarded as "base". The appraisal will need to be carried out through careful consultation with the project leaders the individual has worked for, and some effort will be required on the appraiser's part to maintain continuous contact during the period under review.

Employees engaged in repetitive, labour-intensive production tasks are often left out of appraisal schemes because there seems to be little to discuss. The need for such jobs still exists, no matter how much talk there is about job design and enrichment. To leave such employees out of a scheme will only serve to convince them that they are the least valued of the organisation's workforce. Small wonder that they might not worry too much about letting the odd underweight batch through, or the odd screw out of the accessories pack. (If they are not important, the detail they have to attend to cannot be that important either can it?) People in jobs like this invariably have a worthwhile contribution to make. Their views on how things work are worth hearing. Their ideas about the product they deal with could spawn improvements. They deserve recognition for the effort they put into what they do. At worst, there can be agreement that they just want to be left alone to get on with the job, but "thank you for asking anyway!".

A lack of growth in some organisations may mean that very few opportunities open up for people to need new skills or to be developed. These organisations may feel that appraisal is going to indicate that opportunities exist, which in reality are just not there. There is still every good reason to appraise in such circumstances, providing that the constraints are clear to all. Sadly, one or two employees, having realised that there really are no opportunities for them because it has been spelt out beyond doubt during an appraisal discussion, may well decide to leave. Such casualties are regrettable, but the short-term inconvenience has to be weighed up against the long-term problem of a "powder keg" of frustrated and disillusioned employees with the potential to cause all sorts of trouble.

Management Commitment

Often there is a marked lack of commitment on the part of managers to appraising staff. When they say that they do not have the time, what they mean is that it is not important enough. People will always make time for something they *really* want to do, and it is as well to address this problem by stressing benefits, rather than from the "time" angle.

There is sometimes a lack of acceptance that staff development matters are the manager's job, often because, historically, such matters have been placed in the hands of a personnel department. To get managers committed to staff appraisal and development, it is important that it is not merely imposed upon them — there has to be ownership. Managers must be consulted when a scheme is introduced or revised, and their views considered and followed up. Even a scheme that apparently works well should be reviewed regularly and the manager's responsibility for staff development should be re-emphasised.

Most problems in performance appraisal are not insurmountable. Providing that they are faced up to and constraints understood, it is rare not to find some solution so that appraisal will work as well as possible in the given circumstances.

Chapter 5
Conclusion

Summary of Key Points

The Meaning of Performance Appraisal

(a) Performance appraisal is a systematic means of ensuring that managers and their staff meet regularly to agree past and present performance issues, and to agree what future action is appropriate on both sides. Discussion is based on a clear and mutual understanding of the job in question and would normally be on a one-to-one basis between employees and their immediate managers.

(b) Assessment only deals with the past and present. Appraisal differs in that it looks ahead to improve and develop.

(c) Appraisal is not a form-filling exercise designed to achieve little but obtaining a signature from the appraisee.

(d) Appraisal should be a continuous process, formalised on a regular basis so that the review period can be summarised and the months ahead planned constructively. There must be no surprises in an appraisal meeting.

(e) Performance is a matter which needs to be considered both in terms of results achieved and behaviour demonstrated.

(f) Disciplinary matters are best kept separate from the appraisal arena.

(g) Appraisal should not concentrate on personal characteristics. An action plan designed to restructure an individual's personality is impossible to produce and attempts at doing so may be offensive in the extreme.

(h) The focus of an appraisal should be a two-way discussion, with the appraiser acting as a facilitator in reaching agreement. The appraisal form will be an agreed account of the discussion from which a picture of current performance and future actions must be clearly discernible.

(i) Discussion about the future in an appraisal must be realistic. Promises must not be made which the organisation will fail to keep. Individuals' particular needs and aspirations must be considered and the future planned appropriately.

Considering Relevant Objectives for Performance Appraisal

(a) A major step in devising a performance appraisal scheme is to consider what outcomes are required - ie, what objectives will be set.

(b) These objectives must be aligned with the organisation's future aims.

(c) The appraisal scheme must reflect the management style of an organisation. A participative scheme in an extremely autocratic environment will be doomed to failure by virtue of the suspicion it creates and the lack of commitment it generates.

(d) Appraisal should not be introduced as a "cure all" for ill-defined people-management problems. This will do more harm than good since it will create a lot of work which will result in no outcome, other than seriously to damage management credibility.

(e) Appraisal is an excellent opportunity to promote good corporate and one-to-one communications.

(f) Appraisal can only be useful as a communication tool if it is operated as part of an overall climate of good communication. It will create problems of its own if introduced as a substitute for good corporate communication.

(g) It is impossible to generalise when discussing the motivation of staff, since individuals are motivated in many different ways.

(h) Appraisal is relevant to motivating staff in three key areas:

    (i) it is concerned with achievement, recognition, involvement, the creation of job satisfaction and development,

    (ii) it strengthens the manager/staff relationship and gives an opportunity for managers to keep abreast of the changes which occur in people's capabilities and aspirations,

(iii) the goal-setting element of appraisal underpins a management style which encourages people to achieve by giving them the scope and freedom to do so.

(i) For managers who take staff motivation seriously, appraisal is an indispensable tool.

(j) Linking pay to an objective appraisal system can be better than distributing awards by some arbitrary and subjective method.

(k) There may be problems associated with linking pay to appraisal. Employees must be consistently "enabled" to do their jobs if the system is to be fair. Communication about performance is likely to be inhibited, lest appraisees "shoot themselves in the foot".

(l) If a link exists, separating the appraisal and the pay review on the calendar is a workable idea.

(m) Discussing promotion at appraisal is desirable for some employees, although there may be a potential to inhibit honest communication.

(n) Appraisers must always discuss promotional prospects in an honest and realistic light.

(o) To list appraisal alongside such items as health schemes as an employment benefit demonstrates faith in it as an employee "perk".

(p) Raising levels of efficiency in an organisation is a natural outcome of a skilfully implemented appraisal process.

(q) Organisational training needs are best analysed and evaluated in an exercise specifically designed for that purpose. Appraisal should be used to customise needs and decide which training methods are most appropriate for individuals.

(r) Managers must be responsible for the training and development of their staff, and carrying out appraisal reaffirms this aspect of their job.

(s) Appraisal can be used to plan current and future staffing needs, and to examine current job descriptions and working practices. Managers can gain further insight into developing trends which need attention and into their own performance as managers.

(t) Although not a paper-based exercise, appraisal is useful in assisting to keep records of employees' performance for practical purposes.

(u) Appraisal should assist in reducing labour turnover in that it may identify problems which can be resolved before an employee feels compelled to leave.

(v) Considering the objectives of appraisal is to consider its many benefits as they relate to organisations, managers and individuals. Objectives must be meaningful, achievable and consistent with organisational aims. Objectives should not conflict with each other.

Overcoming the Problems of Performance Appraisal

(a) It is important to consider both sides of the argument when considering introducing performance appraisal.

(b) Appraisal is a time-consuming exercise if carried out properly, but should be considered as an investment.

(c) Managers' ability to appraise will inevitably vary throughout the organisation. This emphasises the need for thorough training and monitoring.

(d) Resistance to form filling may be encountered and any paperwork must be "user friendly".

(e) The greatest resistance is often to the use of job descriptions. These are desirable to keep appraisal on an objective footing. Where it is deemed inappropriate to use them, the burden of maintaining objectivity is heavier.

(f) Often, negative attitudes within the organisation, run deep and are difficult to overcome. It is important that something is seen to happen as a result of appraisal, as soon as possible.

(g) Certain problems of structure may create difficulties in carrying out appraisal:
   (i) teams which are geographically disparate,
   (ii) teams that are too big,
   (iii) individuals who work for more than one boss or who move from project to project,
   (iv) certain production jobs may be seen as too basic to warrant appraisal,
   (v) opportunities for development and promotion are sometimes very limited.

(h) A lack of commitment on the part of appraisers should be addressed by stressing benefits and ensuring that managers are consulted as to how their responsibility for staff development can be carried out.

(i) Most problems in implementing performance appraisal are surmountable, providing that they are understood and addressed appropriately.

Part 2

Introducing or Revising a Performance Appraisal Scheme

Chapter 1
Introduction

The decision to introduce or revise a performance appraisal scheme often comes from the most senior levels of an organisation. It can also be a "customer led" initiative, from employees who are aware of the benefits of good communication and participation and who want to have a formalised way of making an impact on their own working lives.

However the decision is arrived at, involving those who will be using the scheme in its construction is paramount to success in implementing it.

There are a great many issues, options and constraints to consider with people before getting a performance appraisal scheme off the ground. Part 2 therefore deals with the practical details of the exercise:

(a) creating the right climate
(b) getting started
(c) formulating objectives
(d) choosing the most appropriate methods
(e) procedural aspects
(f) communication and training.

Chapter 2
Creating the Right Climate

Whether a performance appraisal scheme is being introduced or revised, it is almost certain that some preconceived ideas are going to need to be dealt with, both amongst managers and staff.

If an existing scheme is being revised, the presumption is that there is something not quite right with it, hence the requirement for change. In this situation, some inherent mistrust is inevitable and a great deal of groundwork will be essential to ensure that the new scheme is received with a degree of enthusiasm.

If a completely new system is being set up, there will still be a number of interesting ideas amongst employees as to exactly what they are in for. Everybody knows somebody who knows something about appraisal. More often than not that somebody has imparted the negative aspects to all and sundry. Some employees may even have had firsthand experience, having been part of an appraisal scheme in a former employment. These experiences may have been good or bad, but "barrack room law" will dictate that there is only mileage in gossiping about the "gory bits".

This is not to say that there will not be a wealth of positive feeling too. The knack is to find it and build on it. An insurance company in the north of England recruited a new sales director from a much larger organisation which operated an excellent performance appraisal scheme. His enthusiasm for the idea of introducing a similar scheme into his new company led to his being put in charge of a project to do just that. A particularly credible individual, he was also extremely well liked at all levels in the organisation. He was a good choice to get the scheme off the ground and his ability, coupled with his enthusiasm, was enough to introduce the scheme with the minimum of resistance and to see it run smoothly thereafter.

The key to introducing or revising a performance appraisal scheme successfully is to create ownership from the start. Communicating and consulting with all those likely to be affected should be the norm from inception through to implementation. Whilst unqualified assent and support from the top of the organisation is essential, never let it be said that the whole thing was a bright idea from "upstairs". Conducting the exercise on a basis of mutual respect and agreement will gain the organisational commitment required to make performance appraisal work.

Chapter 3
Getting Started — Consulting Users

Once the decision is made to introduce or revise a performance appraisal scheme, discussing how it will work with those who will be using it is the first step. Consultation meetings with managers to discuss the options in operation are an ideal way of handling this stage. Additionally, particularly where there are trade union agreements or staff associations, a good idea is to get a working party together with representatives drawn from all levels of the organisation. Obviously some sort of expert input will be required before discussions can proceed, so that participants will be clear about what their terms of reference are.

The following is an example of an agenda for a meeting held by a team of managers in order to discuss developing a performance appraisal scheme.

In this case, the meeting was chaired by an external consultant. Sufficient expertise for such a role may be available internally in many organisations.

Developing a Performance Appraisal Scheme

OBJECTIVES By the end of the meeting, participants will be able to:

(a) define the objectives of appraisal and outline its benefits
(b) outline the considerations which must be taken into account when implementing an appraisal scheme
(c) consider objectively the pros and cons of the various methods of appraisal
(d) initiate the design of an appraisal system most suited to the needs of the company.

Programme:

9.00	Introduction and objectives
9.30	Appraisal — what and why?

- what is an appraisal and what does an appraisal scheme set out to achieve?
- the difference between assessment and appraisal
- appraisal in context (management style; motivation; communication)

10.45	Coffee
11.00	The considerations of introducing an appraisal scheme

- what the company wishes to achieve
- the constraints
- the practical implementation of the scheme

1.00	Lunch
2.00	Methods of appraisal

- a consideration of some methods of appraising staff in relation to their suitability for the company

3.30	Tea
3.45	Developing an appraisal system for the company

- the intention of this session is to commence the design of an appraisal scheme best suited to the company

5.00	Close of day

The idea of consultation is not to form a popular consensus as to what everyone thinks is a good idea. A co-ordinator with experience and know-how needs to structure discussions, correlate views, offer an initial draft for further comment and produce a final design which demonstrates that users' input has been respected and utilised where appropriate. This person may also become the co-ordinating officer once the scheme is in full swing. Introducing a scheme in this way should also assist in achieving consistency in approach when managers come to carry out their appraisals. Having been a party to the decision-making process, everyone should be aware of what the demands of the scheme are going to be and should be committed to meeting them.

Chapter 4
Formulating Objectives

A set of objectives which are clearly relevant to organisational objectives must be the next stage of the process in introducing a new or revised performance appraisal scheme.

How appraisal relates to the various aspects of management and how it strengthens these aspects has been dealt with at some length in Part 1, but introducing an appraisal scheme is not a panacea that will improve things in general if no specific purpose is highlighted. Therefore a set of stated aims is essential. The ultimate goals of the scheme are necessary considerations in how it will be implemented. If an objective is to improve communication, it will be a participative scheme. If another objective is to enhance efficiency, it will deal with setting, achieving and improving standards of work.

When it comes to communicating these objectives to employees, terms with which they can identify should be used. The corporate good may be the overall aim of the appraisal scheme but the question "How does it affect me?" from staff is an inevitable one. It follows that any set of objectives would do well to focus on benefits to the individual, whilst making it clear that these will lead to benefits for the organisation.

The following is an example of a set of objectives written into an appraisal procedures manual for managers. (A simpler version of this was produced for the staff handbook.)

The Objectives of the Company's Appraisal Scheme

The Company appraisal scheme has been designed to meet three specific objectives. The first is to assist all staff in performing their job to the best of their ability, thus maximising their job satisfaction and, naturally, their contribution to the Company's objectives. The principal tool in achieving this first objective is a careful examination of the job carried out by each member of staff using a job description, and an objective assessment of individuals' strengths and weaknesses relating to performance in that job. By utilising strengths fully, and taking positive action to improve weaker areas, the intention is that every member of staff is given the opportunity to perform to their fullest potential, and get the most from their work.

The second objective is to identify training needs. This objective will be pursued in two ways. First, individuals' particular training needs and the specific methods of training required are highlighted by the assessment of performance in each part of their job. Second, more widespread or "global" training needs are highlighted by the co-ordinated feedback resulting from carrying out performance appraisals with staff throughout the organisation.

The third objective is to identify the potential that certain individuals may have to develop in the job that they are already doing, or to develop towards other jobs within the Company. This may even involve progression into more senior posts. Whilst the assessment of performance is important in this area, the aspirations of the individuals concerned need to be explored in the context of this objective, and direction towards development specifically planned and followed up.

It is recognised that not all three objectives will apply equally to every member of staff, but it will be the Company's policy to ensure that every individual is appraised on a yearly basis, and that an exchange of views will take place between job holders and their managers, at an appraisal interview. The summary of this interview is intended to represent the continuous dialogue between managers and staff throughout the preceding year, and should also be considered as the starting point of good communications during the coming year.

The benefits of appraisal in terms of improved communication and enhanced performance both for individuals and for the Company, will only be achieved by the consistent commitment of all those concerned with the scheme.

Chapter 5
Designing a Performance Appraisal Scheme — the Options

Since the design of a performance appraisal scheme will be determined by its aims, it is important to consider carefully the range of options available. At one extreme, if all that is required is a single rating so that pay awards can be distributed, a form setting out scoring against certain criteria is sufficient. There is not even any need for the appraisee to see the form.

At the other extreme, if the objectives are as set out in the example on page 46, a participative method will be used which creates ample opportunity for discussion in the relevant areas. The appraisal report form will contain a number of prompts which complement the objectives of the scheme. In this case there would be sections on performance related to job requirements, particular strengths and weaknesses, action plans, training requirements, and interest in future development.

To remain true to the definition of appraisal offered in Part 1, some of the options about to be discussed might not be considered as performance appraisal. However, in the interests of providing a comprehensive analysis of the methods available, a number of traditional and progressive approaches will be examined.

Who Will be Appraised?

A scheme which is designed to include only particular sections of the workforce will have problems from the outset. If senior members of staff deem themselves to be "above" being appraised or if more junior employees are not considered worth appraising, the scheme will seem to be divisive and potentially unfair. Granted, appraisal may have certain different characteristics at the various levels of the organisation because demands and constraints may be different. This does not alter the fact that every member of the organisation, from the most senior to the most junior, should be embraced by an appraisal scheme which is consistently and fairly applied at all levels.

Open or Closed?

This is the broadest of options. Either the appraisal scheme is open and employees know what is on their appraisal report form, or it is closed and they do not. There seems very little point in the latter, since its only virtue is that it is quick. Clearly the more desirable of the two options is the former, since it means that feedback of a sort has taken place and can be acted upon. Managers have to account for what they say and take much more care about objectivity and accuracy.

Management Led or Joint?

A management-led appraisal scheme is one where the managers in an organisation call all the shots. They decide what is to be said, when to say it and usually invite no more than a signature on a form which has been filled in prior to the meeting (if such a meeting even takes place). This can be done with the minimum of effort on the manager's part and all the employee is required to do, by way of preparation, is to check how his or her name is spelt! Outcomes in an exercise like this are minimal, since any action to be taken has been decreed by the manager, meaning that the employee has little commitment to it and will probably not see it through.

A joint approach in performance appraisal is more in keeping with its real purpose — to discuss and agree past, present and future performance standards. Both appraisers and appraisees prepare the matters which they wish to discuss, arrange to sit down together at an appraisal meeting, agree on how the previous review period has gone and jointly plan objectives for the coming review period. This option could be said to be management steered, rather than management led.

A third runner in this field is shared appraisal. Broadly speaking, this facilitates two-way assessments — managers assess their staff and staff assess their managers. This is certainly a democratic approach but would seem to confuse the issue of exactly who managers have to be accountable to for their standards of performance. Complications would arise when unpopular decisions have to be made by managers and it should not be overlooked that many appraisees are unlikely to be trained and objective assessors. There is a certain organisation which considers employees' appraisals of their managers when allocating the management salary review — a potential opportunity for revenge!

Personality, Performance or Conduct?

There are three possibilities in choosing what aspects to discuss in an appraisal scheme: performance related to job requirements, conduct and personality traits. Part 1 has already examined the constraints of each of these possibilities. The following example is part of an appraisal form from a scheme which incorporates all three.

Illustration 1

Employee Performance Review

Conduct at work   *Rating (A B C)*
Compliance with company rules
Punctuality
Attendance
Appearance

Attitudes
Loyalty
Commitment
Teamwork
Initiative

Quality of work
Accuracy
Speed
Presentation

Personal Qualities
Co-operation
Resilience
Politeness and cheerfulness

In this particular example, much emphasis has been placed on conduct since it is the first item on the list. The two sections dealing with ill-defined immeasurables (ie, attitudes and personal qualities) are a gift to the manager who would like to indulge in a subjective and unquantifiable character assassination. Much would depend on the appraiser's interpretation of the words used. Indeed, there is a natural tendency for people to use themselves as the benchmark for another person's attributes and judge by their own standards. The chemistry between individuals is also significant here — dislike, mutual or otherwise, could lead to some damning outcomes in a system like this one.

There are numerous examples of similar appraisal forms, demonstrating schemes which concentrate only briefly on performance. Therefore, by definition, these are not strictly speaking performance appraisal schemes. There is no denying that conduct and certain personal qualities are relevant to job performance. The discussion of these elements is therefore best conducted in the context of reaching standards of performance. This will assist in keeping the exercise objective and, more importantly, will create scope for positive action to assist in reaching targets.

The following is an example of part of an appraisal form from a scheme which asks for key areas of the job to be specified, assessments to be agreed in each of them, and action plans to be noted where relevant. (Only a small segment is shown here. The appraiser could use as many sheets as required in order to ensure that all items were covered comprehensively.)

Illustration 2

Confidential Appraisal Form (page 2)

Summary of performance in relation to each key area of job description, and actions agreed where appropriate.

Key area	Comments	Action Plan

Rating or Narrative?

Whatever elements are to be evaluated as part of the appraisal scheme, a method of recording assessments and decisions has to be chosen. This choice is basically between narrative or rating. Examples of a rating form and a narrative form are shown in Illustrations 1 and 2 respectively in the previous section.

Rating

Rating is quick, simple and easy to refer back to. This is particularly useful if the appraisal is to be linked to a pay review. The problems of rating, however, considerably outweigh its advantages.

(a) There is a natural tendency for managers to play safe and go for a middle rating. In a grid with an odd number of columns, the middle one will be favoured; in a grid with an even number of columns, the middle two will be favoured. Opting for the top grade seems difficult for some appraisers, since it may indicate that there is no room for improvement. Opting for the bottom grade is just as tricky and often very confrontational.

　　Not all rating-system forms are filled in in advance and then simply shown to appraisees. Some schemes insist that the rating is jointly agreed between the appraiser and appraisee. However, even with this approach there is a danger that appraisees feel that they have been "labelled" if such words as "acceptable" or "satisfactory" have been used to describe them. A retail organisation, noted for the quality of its bananas, used a rating system in its appraisal scheme. A member of staff was heard to say, as he came out of his manager's office after his appraisal, that he felt like a rejected banana!

　　Research also shows that these labels tend to stick. Dramatic changes between one appraisal and the next have to take place before appraising managers will consider replacing the old label, with a new and more complimentary one.

(b) Interpretation of grades by managers is often inconsistent across an organisation. Brief qualifying words such as "good", "average" or "poor", may accompany the numbers or letters which head the columns in the rating grid. It is these which cause the problems of interpretation and compound the difficulties of attaching labels. .

Employees' interpretations can be just as suspect as those of their managers. If an appraisee is labelled as satisfactory, then that would seem to indicate an acceptable standard. Most people, however, would consider being rated merely "satisfactory" or "acceptable" as something of an insult. If such grades are simply shown to appraisees, confrontation is a likely outcome. Even if grades are discussed, it would be quite difficult to gain agreement in establishing an "insulting" grade.

(c) The problem of interpretation in a grading system is often addressed by the formulation of a set of descriptions which exemplify performance in the elements being appraised.

For example:

CUSTOMER SERVICE CLERK

Key area	A *Excellent*	B *Good*	C *Fair*	D *Poor*
Handling customer enquiries on the telephone.	Always answers enquiries positively and takes necessary follow-up action.	Usually answers enquiries promptly and efficiently.	Answers enquiries as required but offers no more than minimum of assistance.	Is frequently unhelpful and slow in dealing with enquiries.

This approach does give more guidance and therefore more consistency in use, but it does assume that a whole range of possibilities can be neatly squeezed into a limited number of forced choices. The problem of attaching labels is still not obviated.

(d) Creating an overall rating, if such a thing is necessary, by counting up or averaging out "scores" often gives a misleading picture. If a number of factors are assessed, the chances are that they do not have an equal impact on the job. Using the example above, the key area illustrated would probably be one of the most important in the job description. A key area dealing with something like "ordering stationery", would be relevant but not as vital to success in the job.

An "A" for ordering stationery, and a "C" for handling customer enquiries would indicate that performance needed considerable improvement. The other way round, would only mean an adjustment to filling in an order form.

This problem can be overcome by giving the factors assessed an appropriate weighting so that a more accurate picture of performance in relation to the job's main purpose would be obtained.

Narrative

Narrative, to be meaningful, must address specifics. An unstructured description of overall performance is unlikely to be objective enough or sufficiently detailed to extract any clear direction for the future.

To be helpful, narrative has to be structured by the provision of a number of relevant prompts such as "What are main strengths?" or "Consider performance in relation to the key areas outlined in the job description".

This form of narrative is time-consuming and demanding, and if simply pushed across the desk for the appraisee to read, potentially regarded just as much "labelling" as the rating technique. Some skill in the written word is necessary and it is not hard to imagine appraisers sitting up all night screwing up endless attempts at writing down what they are trying to convey.

The best way to approach narrative is for appraisers and appraisees to agree on a brief summary of what has been said during an interview in relation to each prompt. This summary can then be reproduced, probably after the interview itself, on the appraisal form. It is not unheard of for appraisees to be given the job. Since both parties will see the report and agree its accuracy before signing it, it does not matter who actually puts pen to paper. Accuracy in this case refers to accuracy of reporting. Debate over accuracy in assessing performance may be part of what is recorded. The report is signed to acknowledge that it is an accurate record of the discussion. Ideally, agreement will have been reached. If it is not, that fact must also be recorded and further action on the matter highlighted. Style is never as important as content in an appraisal report form but this approach does mean that the appraiser will not have to pore over the right choice of words so as not to offend or embarrass the appraisee.

Frequency and Timing

How Often?

Appraisal is a time-consuming process and, since it is ideally an ongoing management function, a summary once or twice a year is likely to be a big enough commitment. It is better for it to be carried out well at long intervals, than poorly, more frequently.

Timing

Some organisations will choose a particular time of year to carry out appraisals which may or may not have some relationship with the timing of salary reviews. This approach is useful, since appraisal feedback can be monitored to identify more easily any widespread themes which may emerge. Appraisers find it useful to get into appraisal "mode", in the same way that they might concentrate their attentions on budgeting or a peak sales period, at given times.

This approach will also ensure some pattern in the order in which appraisals take place. Some organisations choose to start at the top and work down so that every appraiser will have been appraised. It would be reasonable to expect that certain points arising from managers' appraisals would affect the action plans of their staff. An example might be a manager who has been exhorted to delegate more – it would follow that the targets set for that manager's staff would contain some delegated tasks. Managers will need to be assessed as appraisers at some point, but since the appraisals which they have carried out should be passed on to their boss for review, this can be done at this stage.

Starting at the bottom and working up is an alternative to the above but its only virtue would probably be the fact that the extra meeting to appraise the appraiser would not be necessary.

A number of organisations endeavour to spread the appraisal workload by arranging interviews to be carried out on or around employees' anniversary of engagement, or anniversary of appointment to their current position. This certainly allows the manager to give each subject individual attention, but it may become a cumbersome monthly ritual. A large retail organisation switched to this method, but found that since many staff joined it in November and December as temporary seasonal workers, most appraisals needed to be done at the busiest time of year!

It is also difficult to identify more widespread themes when using this approach since they will emerge only very gradually and perhaps too slowly for any plans to be laid which will indicate that the appraisal process is producing some positive outcomes.

Choosing an Option

It is quite possible to have any combination of the aforementioned options. Some combinations are naturally more cohesive than others. Some would not sit well together at all. For example, an organisation could use a closed management-led narrative, where managers spend a great deal of time on writing out what they think of their staff's performance and then file the report. The only objective that this approach would meet would be that of recording. It is not particularly useful for salary awards, since narrative does not always give a concise enough summary of performance. It will be one sided, probably very subjective and would achieve very little considering all the time it would take.

An alternative might be an open, joint rating of personality traits. The idea of having to pick over the bones of one's personality with the boss is an undignified prospect for most people. Even if the ratings which are finally recorded have been reached by discussion, there is not much that can be done with the information to improve performance.

The above examples serve only to illustrate the point and in reality are unlikely to be in popular use. Experience has shown, that one of the most productive combinations of all the options is an open system, where agreements are reached about elements of performance and future action, and a written summary of the discussion is produced for continued reference.

Appraisal Forms

Whilst appraisal is not meant to be a paper-based exercise, carefully constructed appraisal forms will assist in ensuring that the scheme is used with some consistency throughout the organisation, and that there is something to refer back to.

Because objectives are so important in determining form design it is not possible to provide any sort of template purporting to be the perfect model. Paperwork would also need to be in keeping with the usual house style and image of the organisation using it.

The following is intended only to be a guide as to what might be included in a form which supports an open, joint scheme and which focuses on reviewing and improving performance.

Preparation Forms

A "preparation for appraisal" form which employees will be given approximately two weeks before their interview is to be held is a useful feature in appraisal documentation. A space to state the time and date is a good practical addition to this form and attaching a copy of the job description and/or previously agreed action plans is also desirable to emphasise the basis for discussion. This form should complement the appraisal form itself in that it will provide similar prompts for discussion (eg a consideration of strengths or weaknesses, factors affecting perform-ance, aspirations or interests, action required to assist future perform-ance). Certain questions will encourage appraisees to think about how they are managed and resourced, for example, "What further support do you need?" or "What obstacles have prevented you from achieving ob-jectives?".

Inviting a complete self-appraisal is frequently a feature of preparation forms. This is quite a challenging and often unwelcome demand for some employees, although useful in establishing the size of the task in reaching agreement. People rarely like to set themselves up to be contradicted and complete objectivity about oneself is almost impossible, so this idea does have limitations.

Some organisations include space on the preparation form for ap-praisees to fill in for themselves a current job description or a résumé of current objectives. This approach is admirable for jobs which are flexible and tend to change or develop rapidly, usually at more senior levels. Where more basic process jobs rely on conformity and consistency of application, this approach would be less appropriate, although employees' views on their jobs are always helpful.

A question about the current validity of a job description would indicate the value placed on the job holder's views. It would be vital to point out, however, that any comments made would have to be considered in perspective and change would not necessarily follow as a matter of course.

If the use of formal job descriptions is not the norm for the organisation, asking employees to write down their perceptions of their job responsibilities is a useful way of structuring the eventual interview and of finding out what people think their job is about.

It should be noted whether completing the form and returning it is mandatory or voluntary. Some employees, particularly less senior ones, will be horrified at the prospect of presenting their written skills for inspection in such a way. The approach taken regarding the return of the preparation form will need to be considered in the light of each appraisee's capabilities and preferences.

The Appraisal Form

As to the appraisal report form itself, a fairly simple structure is best. This will be a particularly useful feature in enabling the form to be used across all the categories in the organisation. Different types of appraisal at different levels can be a very divisive approach, and not at all helpful in promoting the harmonisation of working conditions and practices.

The form should prompt a logical examination of the issues relevant to the appraisees' current levels of performance and potential for the future. There should be plenty of space in all sections.

The first item could invite a summary of all matters relating to performance against an up-to-date job description and previously agreed standards and targets. Following on from this, plans for training and development could be requested. An examination of aspirations and potential for development should be included and of course there has to be an "any other business" section.

The "any other business" section should in fact be superfluous, since, as in any other type of meeting, the prepared agenda should be comprehensive and specific. Nevertheless, it should be included to facilitate discussion not prompted by other means.

Finally, a separate sheet, detailing a summary of objectives and action plans would be practical; this would form a concise working document for the use of appraiser and appraisee, so that follow-up can be monitored without the risk of the whole appraisal form being passed around for everyone to see.

Not all parts of the appraisal form would have to be filled in for every appraisee. A tendency often surfaces for forms to be viewed rather like crossword puzzles, in that to achieve success, every space has to be filled in. There will always be staff who are getting along reasonably well and have no wish to change anything. The key to success in completing appraisal forms is honesty, accuracy and appropriateness.

There should, of course, be a space for signatures at the end of the form (side by side is a good touch, denoting that the whole exercise has been a joint effort). A space at the very end asking for the reviewing manager's comments should not be used for further analysis of the appraisee unless he or she is present. This section serves a practical function by providing an assurance that the appraisal has been reviewed by the relevant third party. Any comments on it are bound not to be particularly meaningful in the context of the appraisal itself. Reviewing managers may well use a copy of the form which does not go back to the appraisee, to record discussions on the manager's capabilities as an appraiser.

On the subject of copies, three is more than enough. The top copy goes to the appraisee who is, after all, the most important person in the process. The second copy needs to be kept securely by the appraiser as a working copy, and the last one can form the personnel file copy once it has passed through the hands of the reviewing manager.

If this type of appraisal is to be used for salary awards, there must be a space on it somewhere for an overall summary or grading, which the appraisee should be aware of. No matter how objective the appraisal has been, there is bound to be a degree of subjectivity in applying this final judgment and possibly the best that can be hoped for if this has to be done is that at least the summary or grading can be an agreed one, based on the discussion which preceded its being recorded.

The following form is in current use by a medium-sized company with jobs which range from very creative activities to repetitive processes.

Private and confidential

Preparation for appraisal

Employee's Name: ....

Job Title: ....

It is recommended that you use this form to help you think about the job you do, prior to your interview, the date and time of which is: ....

1. What parts of the job do you feel you do well?

2. What parts of the job do you have difficulties with, and are there any obstacles which have caused you particular problems?

3. What training (if any) do you feel you need? What further support (if any) do you feel you need?

4. Are there any other areas of your department or the Company in which you are interested?

5. Are there any other points which you would like to raise at your appraisal?

Private and confidential

Annual appraisal   *Page 1*

Name .... Department ....

Job Title .... Supervisor/Manager ....

Length of time in current position ....

1. List key areas of the job, highlighting strengths and skills that have
    contributed to performance during the appraisal review period.

2. What aspects of performance could be improved? Detail how this is to be achieved.

3. *Development and training*

    a) Consider future potential and development, in particular highlighting specific areas for training.

    b) Are there any other areas of the department or the Company in which an interest has been expressed?

4. In the light of this appraisal, identify any changes to the key areas of the job description and make recommendations for any appropriate amendments.

a) Appraiser's comments

b) Employee's comments

I hereby confirm that this is a fair and accurate representation of the appraisal discussion.

SIGNATURE: Appraisee ....Appraiser ....

DATE: ....

SIGNATURE: Reviewing Manager ....

3 copies   - 1 to appraisee
           - 1 to appraiser
           - 1 to personnel file

Agree a plan for the forthcoming year (wherever possible). A time-scale of action and results to be achieved should be agreed where appropriate.

Key areas and standard of performance or further objectives	Action plan to be followed	Target date for review

Chapter 6
Procedural Aspects

Regular appraisal is not an employment "right". However, if it operates within an organisation, certain obligations will have to be observed, both legal and ethical.

Confidentiality

An appraisal remains confidential within certain limits in the organisation. Typically, this might extend to appraisee, appraiser, appraiser's manager and the co-ordinating officer. Co-ordination can be carried out by the personnel department, the company secretariat or by a senior manager. Clerical staff carrying out filing procedures must be aware that appraisals are not available for inspection by them. Any breach of this might even be considered as a disciplinary matter.

Ensuring Fairness and Co-ordinating Feedback

Total objectivity is virtually an impossible demand but every attempt must be made to operate the appraisal scheme as fairly as possible. Offering appraisals for review by the next level of management does give the opportunity for a third party to provide an impartial overview and should be an integral part of the system. Additionally, a senior person in the organisation should monitor the entire system. These two levels of review are also essential for co-ordinating feedback.

Equal Opportunities

Nothing about an appraisal scheme should be discriminatory. Any restrictions imposed upon an employee, for instance in consideration for development or access to training opportunities, on the grounds of race or sex, are contrary to the provisions of the Race Relations Act 1976 and the Sex Discrimination Act 1975. The appraisal scheme must reflect the organisation's overall obligation to maintain an equal oppportunities climate.

A trade union, at its annual conference, highlighted the problems of appraisal schemes which use personality traits as a basis for assessment. This method is particularly prone to a discriminatory approach. In the cited examples, men were described by words such as "efficient" and women were described by such words as "well-groomed".

The message from this example is that using actual job performance as the basis for assessment is much safer from this point of view. The Commission for Racial Equality recommends this approach.

Getting this aspect wrong could lead employees to exercise their right to make a complaint to an industrial tribunal. Appraisal forms and procedures may be used by employees as evidence in support of their claim that discrimination has taken place.

The equal opportunities dimension is a good reason to operate the same type of appraisal scheme throughout the organisation. A scheme operated uniformly provides no grounds for allegations that its very structure is discriminatory.

The Data Protection Act 1984

Employees have a right to see any personal data relating to them which is held on a computer system. This would only be a consideration in a closed scheme if all information is entered on to computerised personnel records. For organisations operating an open scheme, this legislation is of no particular consequence and this is another good reason for operating a system in which employees do not have to resort to the law in order to find out how they are "rated".

Disciplinary Procedures

Whilst never to be used as a substitute disciplinary mechanism, an appraisal must reflect an accurate picture of performance. In the event of dismissal for poor performance and a claim being made that the sacking was unfair, the employer's case will not be enhanced if the appraisal contradicts the content of the disciplinary meetings.

Appeals

The procedures relating to the appraisal scheme, as communicated to employees, should refer to an opportunity to appeal if they are not satisfied with how the exercise has been carried out. This appeal could be the normal grievance procedure already in operation.

Problems should be resolved in a more positive way than this. If the appraisal report is an accurate record of the discussion which took place, rather than a summary of the manager's views, the potential for conflict is greatly reduced. If the appeals procedure is used frequently, management must consider this as a very clear alarm that the appraisal system is suffering some abuse.

Paperwork and Administration

The issue and storage of all paperwork must be in the hands of a part of the organisation which can efficiently control it. This would cover all aspects such as:

(a) stationery stocks
(b) issue of forms or reminders that appraisals are due
(c) dates by which appraisals must be completed
(d) storage of the file copies of the appraisal forms
(e) production of any resultant data.

This is possibly one of the least desirable responsibilities in the operation of an appraisal scheme but it is vitally important that the system is efficiently operated to maintain its credibility and momentum.

The following is an example of the procedural details included in a set of guidelines for managers.

Notes on procedures

(a) Appraisal interviews will normally take place once a year, between 1 June and 31 July. Staff would, except in special circumstances, usually be interviewed by their immediate manager on a one-to-one basis.

(b) Exceptions to the above will be new employees or new post holders. These members of staff will normally have an appraisal in the month prior to completing their first six months in the job. Thereafter, they would join the normal pattern of appraisal interviews as appropriate.

(c) The Administration Manager will, on the appropriate date, send out a reminder that appraisal interviews are due to be carried out, and the date by which forms are to be completed. A list, detailing staff eligible to be appraised by each manager will accompany this reminder.

Appraisal forms can be drawn from stock on receipt of the administrative details.

(d) Prior to the appraisal interviews commencing each year, managers will meet with their staff informally to remind them that appraisals are due and to restate the objectives of the company scheme.

(e) Each member of staff will be given their own preparation for appraisal form approximately two weeks before their interview is scheduled. This will be accompanied by a copy of their job description and a brief personal reminder about the objectives of the appraisal and how the preparation form may be used. (This may be a verbal exercise if preferred.)

(f) All appraisal interviews will take place in private and will remain uninterrupted except in extreme circumstances.

(g) Appraisal forms will be completed by managers after the interview takes place and a short follow-up meeting takes place within five working days, to review and sign the form. There will be three copies of the final form:
    (i)   one for the appraisee to retain
    (ii) one for the manager to use as a working copy
    (iii) one to go to the reviewing manager(s) and eventually to the personal file.

(h) The appeal procedure for staff who are unhappy about the outcome of their appraisal interview will be the same as the appeals procedure relating to grievance, set out in the Staff Handbook.

(i) Two senior members of the company's management will review all appraisals to ensure consistency in the application of the scheme, and to identify any requirements that emerge across the organisation. All appraisals will remain confidential within these limits.

(j) Following the appraisal review each year, managers will be asked to consider the application of the scheme and report to a managers' meeting designed to review and improve all aspects of it for the future.

Chapter 7
Communication and Training

Communication

From the very outset, if an appraisal scheme is being revised or introduced, effective communication with those who will be affected by it, must be a priority. Even at the discussion stage, if managers and representatives attend meetings, word will get round that something is afoot. It is better for employees to be told the right thing by the right people at the right time, than to hear distorted information through the grapevine. The misinterpretation and speculation which results from the grapevine method of communication will not assist in the smooth introduction of the new appraisal scheme.

At a later stage, when the scheme is about to be implemented, its intentions must be communicated clearly from the top of the organisation down. By far the most effective method of doing this will be face-to-face meetings between managers and their staff, which invite discussion and get feedback. Managers must be well prepared for these meetings and know enough about the background and objectives of the scheme to be able to cope with their staff's natural concerns.

Newsletters or memos to all staff from the chief executive are desirable in order to demonstrate commitment from the top but should never be a substitute for face-to-face meetings. The opportunity to offer views and ask questions is essential for staff who wish to give the new scheme a good chance of succeeding for them.

The briefing must of course be consistent across the organisation, although managers may wish to add a little "local" information, such as where they might hold their interviews or when they are planning to get started. Another feature of the briefing must be that it is completely honest! For example, if there is to be a connection between appraisal and reward, however remote, then this must be revealed in the briefing.

Communication cannot stop at the introductory stages of the appraisal scheme. The staff handbook or information package should include a section on it, and an induction programme would need some further material to support this. Reminders each year, preferably in face-to-face meetings, are essential to maintain the momentum of the scheme and to ensure that all staff still perceive the objectives of the scheme accurately, and with some faith.

A further aspect of the communication process is facilitating some feedback from users when the appraisal round has been completed each year. Care should be taken not to react too strongly to natural teething problems which will be resolved anyway, but all comments should be followed up and considered to demonstrate that the scheme can be constructively influenced by its "owners".

Training Appraisers

Each and every individual who is responsible for interviewing in an appraisal situation *must* have some training. This training should include not only the interpersonal skills required, but some input on what the appraisal scheme is trying to achieve. Attitude changing may be an important aspect of this training for some people.

Thorough training should ensure some consistency in the application of the appraisal scheme, although of course it is inevitable that certain managers are going to have more skill and commitment than others.

The following is an example of a one day training course designed to develop skills in interviewing. A longer course would be required if more input was required on other aspects such as management style, the benefits of appraisal or motivational issues. The more role plays and case studies trainees do, the better, so a longer course would be required to allow for this. Often a follow-up half-day or so at a later date is more useful. It gives trainees an opportunity to assimilate what they have learnt and to prepare themselves more adequately for some realistic interviewing practice.

Appraisal Interviewing

OBJECTIVES   By the end of the course, delegates will be able to:

(i)   prepare comprehensively and to carry out an appraisal interview with a member of staff

(ii) demonstrate the essential skills required in interviewing in an appraisal situation

(iii) set appropriate targets and carry out the required follow-up to the appraisal.

Programme:

9.00	Introduction and objectives
9.30	Recapping the aims and benefits of an appraisal scheme
10.00	The steps to effective appraisal

Step 1 — Defining jobs
- considering job content to make objective and accurate assessments, and to plan for the future where appropriate

10.30	Coffee
10.45	Step 2 — Preparation

- the preparation which needs to be done by the manager and the appraisee
- group case study

Step 3 — The interview and completing documentation
- the techniques of good interviewing
- the skills of structuring, questioning, listening, probing, joint problem solving, summarising and gaining agreement
- taking notes
- writing up the form comprehensively
- micro case studies

1.00	Lunch
2.00	Step 4 — Planning action and target setting

- identifying action which needs to be taken by appraiser and appraisee
- defining what is target/objective setting
- considering targets to improve performance or enhance skills where appropriate

Step 5 — Follow-up
- ensuring action agreed is implemented by the manager and appraisee
- the manager's credibility
- following up and monitoring the individual's progress after the appraisal

3.00   Tea
3.15   Role plays
        –   each course member will prepare and carry out interviews based on
            a selection of case studies
5.00   Summary of course and close

Note — a well-chosen film will always be helpful and a lively addition to
the proceedings.

Role plays are an essential aid to developing skills but often difficult to get
trainees to do well because of their dislike of such "games". The best role
plays are constructed by the trainees themselves so that they can work
through some of their main areas of concern. However, the course leader
should have one or two "cameos" tucked away for those who "just cannot
think of anything".

The training should be backed up by a comprehensive handbook
which, although it will be faithful to the course content, should also stand
on its own as a reference point. Ideally, retraining should be offered
regularly, but if this is not possible or certain managers miss out on
training for some reason, the handbook must be good enough to "survive"
on.

Evaluating appraisal training "on the ground" is not as straightforward
as normal evaluation. Since appraisal interviews should be a private
matter between managers and their staff, evaluation cannot be carried out
by observation. The appraisal report has to be the most useful source of
information, so its review by senior levels is vital from this, as well as many
other, angles. Eliciting appraisees' views on how they feel about how their
appraisal was carried out could be a dangerous or subjective method of
evaluation. No doubt, however, senior managers would hear soon enough
if there were problems.

A cautionary note on the training of managers in appraisal techniques
would be useful here. All the above is written on the assumption that
managers have been trained to be managers in the first place. Appraisal is
only one aspect of the job and unless it is taught in that context it will have
little impact. Managers' capabilities, both as managers and appraisers, will
always vary throughout an organisation but the want of sound training
initiatives should not be allowed to scupper the newly introduced appraisal scheme.

Training Appraisees

To complete the training process, some time should be invested in the instruction of appraisees. Appraisers will not be able to do a good job if their subjects do not know the "rules of the game".

This does not have to be such a thorough affair as for appraisers, but it is an exercise which will pay off in terms of the scheme's success. Explaining objectives, going through paperwork and suggesting helpful ways to prepare for interviews is what is required. If a certain amount of attitude changing is necessary, such training will go some way to achieving it. Once employees understand that they are about to enter a two-way communication process and that it is recognised that they have much to offer on the subject of how their jobs are performed, they will be much keener to assist the appraisal scheme in reaching its objectives.

Chapter 8
Conclusion

Summary of Key Points

Creating the Right Climate

(a) There will be a number of preconceived ideas at all levels about what performance appraisal means and these must be dealt with.

(b) If revising a scheme, problems with the existing one could lead to inherent mistrust about any changes which might be afoot.

(c) Where no scheme exists at all, it is likely that the grapevine will carry some "interesting", and often fairly negative, speculation into all corners of the organisation.

(d) Find pockets of enthusiasm and build on them.

(e) Create ownership right from the start by communicating with and involving all who will be affected.

(f) There must be commitment from the top, but the idea should not be seen to have been imposed.

(g) Conducting the exercise on a basis of mutual respect and agreement will gain the organisational commitment required to make performance appraisal work.

Getting Started — Consulting Users

(a) Consultation meetings with managers or working parties consisting of appropriate representatives are an ideal way to get the ball rolling.
(b) An experienced and knowledgeable hand needs to guide consultation into a final design which demonstrates that users' input has been respected and utilised where appropriate.
(c) Consulting users in making the decisions assists in achieving a consistency of approach when managers come to carry out their appraisals.

Formulating Objectives

(a) A set of objectives with clear relevance to organisational objectives must be formulated.
(b) Objectives should be specific and be the basis for deciding what options will be used in design and implementation of the appraisal scheme.
(c) When communicating objectives, focus on benefits to the individual before benefits to the organisation. Employees will identify more readily with this approach.

Designing a Performance Appraisal Scheme — the Options

(a) The design of the performance appraisal scheme must enable it to meet its stated objectives.
(b) The appraisal scheme should embrace all levels of staff in a consistent way. There should be no scope to call the scheme divisive.
(c) An open scheme is preferable to a closed one, since feedback and follow-up are necessary to give appraisal some point.
(d) A scheme adopting a joint approach in which managers and staff prepare and discuss performance issues is infinitely preferable to a management-led one, which only requires employees to sign a report about themselves.

   A shared scheme, where managers are also appraised by their staff could confuse authority and accountability.
(e) The three possibilities in choosing what areas to discuss, are personality, performance and conduct. The most productive of the three will be performance since it is the most likely to be objective

and it is possible to build positive action plans for future improvement based on reaching performance standards.

(f) There is a broad choice between rating or narrative when recording appraisals. Rating is quicker but can be very inconsistent and confusing, and therefore inaccurate. Narrative is time-consuming and demanding, and needs to be structured to ensure that it addresses specifics. Narrative is best handled when used to summarise discussions and highlight required action.

(g) Appraisal done well once a year is better than doing it badly several times a year.

(h) Opting for carrying out all appraisals over a short time span does concentrate effort, effect and feedback. This would also allow managers to be appraised from the top down to ensure that forward plans are linked.

Carrying out appraisals over the entire year on anniversaries of appointment does spread the workload but dilutes more general feedback so that positive action resulting from the appraisal scheme is more difficult to implement.

(i) When choosing options in designing a performance appraisal scheme, the various elements should combine well. Experience shows that the most productive combination of the options is an open system where agreements are reached about elements of performance and future action, and a written summary of the discussion is produced for reference.

(j) Although appraisal is not meant to be a paper-based exercise, a well-thought-out form is required to back it up.

(k) The objectives of the appraisal scheme will be reflected in the design of the form. Some useful inclusions for an open, joint scheme which focuses on improving performance might be:
    (i) a preparation form for the appraisee which complements the issues raised by the actual appraisal form
    (ii) an appraisal form with lots of space and logical prompts to ensure discussion on all the relevant points.

Procedural Aspects

(a) The outcomes of appraisal interviews should remain confidential within designated limits.

(b) Reviewing managers and a co-ordinating officer should rationalise all feedback from appraisals and ensure that the scheme is operated fairly and consistently.

(c) The operation of the appraisal scheme should reflect a conscientious equal opportunities policy.

(d) Under the Data Protection Act 1984 employees are entitled to see any personal data, including appraisal reports, held on a computer system. In a scheme which is open anyway, this legislation would have little impact.

(e) Whilst appraisal and discipline must never be confused or substituted, it is important that where disciplinary procedures relating to performance issues are in progress, the appraisal does not give a contradictory picture.

(f) There must be an appeals procedure in place for those who feel that the outcome of their appraisal is unsatisfactory.

(g) Paperwork must be handled by a part of the organisation which can efficiently control it.

Communication and Training

(a) Communication to all those who are affected by the new or revised appraisal scheme must be a priority from the outset.

(b) It is better that employees should get correct information through formal channels, than distorted information through the grapevine.

(c) At the implementation stage, face-to-face briefing meetings from the top of the organisation down are the best way to communicate the intentions of the scheme. These meetings must allow for questions and feedback.

(d) Briefing must be consistent across the organisation and give an honest account of the objectives of the appraisal scheme.

(e) Communication must be continuous, with details readily available in staff handbooks and induction material. Reminders in face-to-face meetings each year are essential to maintain the momentum of the scheme.

(f) An evaluation of the scheme should take place at the appropriate time each year and relevant feedback acted upon.

(g) All appraisers must be trained in the intentions of the appraisal scheme and in the interpersonal skills required.

(h) A training course of appropriate length should be provided and could include sections on management style, the benefits of appraisal and motivational issues, as well as interviewing skills.

(i) A comprehensive handbook should be provided as back-up for the training and as a continuing point of reference.

(j) Appraisal training has to be evaluated by the monitoring of appraisal reports by senior managers.

(k) Appraisal training can only succeed if managers are already trained adequately in other management skills and appraisal is viewed in context.

(l) Appraisee training will enable appraisers to do a better job. Training on objectives, paperwork and preparation will help appraisees understand that appraisal is a two-way process designed to encourage them to offer constructive comments about how their jobs are performed.

Part 3

Carrying Out Performance Appraisal Effectively

Chapter 1
Introduction

The ultimate success of any appraisal scheme, whether it be new, revised or well established, will depend on the effort that goes into putting the whole process into practice. The time it could take to complete a worthwhile appraisal might well be a daunting prospect for busy managers, particularly those who have an unwieldy number of staff.

Equal care at each stage of the process is required and Part 3 will deal with each of those stages:

(a) using job descriptions
(b) preparing for the appraisal meeting
(c) carrying out the appraisal interview
(d) planning future action and
(e) following up.

Chapter 2
Writing or Revising Job Descriptions

In the process of appraising performance, the first step is to consider with staff exactly what they are expected to do and to what standard. The simplest way of doing this is to compile a written list of everything, call it a job description or job definition and ensure that employees have full access to it.

Writing Job Descriptions

How job descriptions are constructed will vary from one organisation to the next, and the chosen format will depend upon the style which the organisation feels is appropriate. At one extreme there will be those who use nothing at all to define jobs because they feel that the depth of knowledge and commitment amongst employees, particularly long-serving ones, will not be enhanced by such a feature. At the other extreme there will be those who define duties in the finest detail, including exactly what standard is to be achieved. Both extremes may suit the organisation using them as long as the situation is reviewed periodically to check the continued relevance of the method.

Job descriptions are useful in a variety of other ways, eg analysing training requirements, in supporting disciplinary procedures, reviewing organisational structure, grading jobs for job evaluation and making the scope of job holders' authority clear.

They will be invaluable in all these areas, providing that they are not allowed to become out of date, and they should be regularly revised as a matter of routine. Appraisal time is a good opportunity to set about doing this, having gained feedback from job holders. Although jobs cannot necessarily be tailored for every individual, there are often cases of jobs changing, growing and offering more to the organisation because of the present incumbent's particular talents.

Whilst there is no particular "right" way to prepare job descriptions, there are some worthwhile points to consider when writing or revising them.

Involving the job holder (assuming that there is one) will capitalise on the fact that those closest to the work are often the best at describing it in the right perspective. Highlighting discrepancies between the job holders' view of the work and that of the boss is one of the most valuable elements of compiling job descriptions in this way. Where it is necessary to cover a number of staff with a common job description all job holders can be consulted, providing that it is understood that contributions will need to be considered in context and a decision made about the final draft by the departmental manager.

The manager does need to exercise considerable objectivity when consulting staff in such a way, for the temptation to leave out the un-popular duties or to over-emphasise the more enjoyable aspects must be recognised. The exercise can be a stern test of the manager's resolve and decision-making ability.

The job description could be constructed as follows:

(a) job title, grades, department
(b) to whom the job holder reports
(c) those people the job holder is responsible for
(d) the overall purpose of the job
(e) the main duties of the job — these could be listed concisely or broken down into key areas, with specific detail noted against each one (this can be more digestible than a long unstructured list in a fairly complex job).

When describing duties it is important to use "action" words. "Liaise with other project managers", would be more pertinent if it said "meet once a week, or more frequently if required, with other project managers". All terminology used should be as straightforward and as free of jargon as possible.

How detailed the "duties" section of the job description should be is a matter of finding the balance between making the description so vague that it is not useful and so detailed that it is complicated and inhibiting.

Consider these three attempts at describing one element of a clerk's job in the claims department of an insurance company.

1. *Responsible for filing.*
   This could mean anything from burning it to spending thousands of pounds on a new system.

2. *Ensure that all departmental filing is maintained in an up-to-date state and is alphabetically and numerically correct.*
   This is much more specific and gives clearer parameters. There is also a reference to the standard required.

3. | **Key Area** | **Duties** |
   |---|---|
   | *Ensure that all departmental filing is maintained in accordance with standing instruction 4:2 in the Operations Manual.* | *File all new claims daily, check weekly that all completed claims are removed and archived, check monthly that all current claims are in correct alphabetical and numerical order.* |

This makes requirements clear by cross-referencing to some standing instructions. However, a great deal of detail is included about how and when the job should be done and it is therefore rather prescriptive. It is likely that much of the detail would be in the standing instruction mentioned.

The amount of detail included is purely a matter of organisational preference. There is a requirement for consistency in style across similar levels of the organisation, although it may be an acceptable refinement to use less prescriptive job descriptions at more senior levels. At this level, or where jobs are changing rapidly, it may be more appropriate to review and agree job objectives at appropriate intervals.

Allocating the percentage of time spent in the various duties is a feature which may be added to some job descriptions. It can be difficult to get such allocations accurate, but if the job description forms part of an evaluation exercise this could be an important determinant in the grading awarded.

Job descriptions, above all things, are meant to help staff, managers and organisations. Too much detail can create problems when something occurs which is not included in anyone's list of duties! Allowing flexibility, by having a section in the job description referring to "any other reasonable task as requested by the job holder's manager" is advisable. Care must be taken not to use this as a licence to slot in something no one else wants to do, or something which was simply forgotten when the job description was compiled. If treated with respect, this facility will encourage some flexibility on the part of the job holder. A job description which is a firm demarcation of who does what and when, is a hindrance, not a help. It should be remembered that if employees keep referring to their job descriptions as a good reason for not doing certain tasks there is a problem related more to management and motivation than to job descriptions.

Standards of Performance

The Need for Standards

Standards are important if there is to be any assessment of performance, whether it is for appraisal purposes or not. There must be some indicators which enable the manager to say whether performance has reached the required standard or to identify a failure. Deciding on a standard of performance may well be a consultation exercise where job holders have been called upon to agree levels of attainment. Further objectives can only be set if a basic standard is recognised and, even then, concise guidelines as to what is required must be indicated. Standards must be clear, measurable and stated in terms of time, quantity or quality. They must also be achievable, preferably with some scope for the job holder to improve even further at a later stage.

Standards are also relevant in setting out guidelines which need to be adhered to for certain practical reasons. Some tasks must be completed within the bounds of safety regulations. There are often aspects of security which need to be observed. Budgetary limits or limits of authority often have to be stated. Deadlines, frequency or timing may need to be indicated. It may be appropriate to indicate minimum quantity or quality levels, or refer to a quality assurance manual.

It is often a problem to set standards where the management style of an organisation is very open. Using rigid guidelines in such circumstances is to impose something quite at variance with the generally accepted ethos. Consultation about standards is likely to be more typical in organisations like this. Whatever approach is used in setting standards, it should be consistent with the normal style of management. However, this style should not compromise clarity or promote ambiguity.

It should also be appreciated that it is simply much easier to set standards in some jobs than in others. Setting a number of key strokes per minute for a VDU operator is not difficult. But how can a reasonable standard be set for someone in a more socially orientated job such as a receptionist? How would helpfulness be quantified in this instance?

The question in fact is "How is helpfulness demonstrated?". Possibly this would be by putting through calls promptly, by taking messages accurately and by assisting visitors to reach their destination without difficulty. By adopting this approach it becomes clearer just how standards can be set even in less systemised types of job.

It is possible that in one job some items are more measurable than others. Managers responsible for output will have very clear production standards available to them, but how do they measure the motivation of staff, for instance? The answer lies in how such a responsibility is defined. Rather than exhort a manager to motivate staff, the duty should be broken down into more tangible items. The following is an example taken from a manager's job description which has been used to communicate standards by incorporating them into the definition of duties:

Key Area	Duties
Motivation of staff	Hold staff meetings at least twice a month as per the "Briefing Policy"; draw up and carry out a training plan for each member of the department according to the Company's training policy, and review its relevance quarterly; appraise staff on a yearly basis according to the procedures laid down in the "Manager's Guide to Appraisal", etc...

Motivation may not be measurable, but it is possible to say whether meetings are held at least twice a month, or whether appraisals are carried out according to the company's guidelines.

Mention of the phrase "standards of performance" can turn the most reasonable people into the most difficult ones. The 40 strong warehousing department of a retailing organisation was the only section of the entire company which was not covered by the appraisal scheme. This situation had arisen because the warehouse staff had instructed their union representatives that they could not accept the "standards of performance" element of the recently introduced job descriptions. The descriptions had been introduced to support the new appraisal scheme in order to ensure that it was applied with scrupulous fairness. Management/staff relations had until this point been extremely harmonious and productive. The outcome of the haggling which ensued was that the job descriptions were withdrawn from the warehouse but so was the appraisal scheme and the merit increases which were linked to it.

Certainly, setting down standards of performance can be fraught with problems, so the greatest care must be taken in establishing them, preferably with a degree of consultation. However, worse problems will arise if employees are assessed and appraised against vague requirements that they are not adequately aware of.

Communicating Standards

As important as setting standards of performance is communicating them adequately so that no one is in any doubt at all about what is required of them. The job description is as suitable a vehicle as any for this purpose.

An education organiser was criticised at her first appraisal interview for not having reached the target increase of students enrolling for classes in her area for that year. She asked what the target increase was, and the answer was "Never less than five per cent". "Where is this written down?" she asked; "How was I supposed to know?". The answer was given that everyone knew it should be about five per cent. It had been that way for a long time and it was just an understanding amongst the organisers that this was the increase they were expected to achieve. The discussion was enough to make the manager realise without any further examination, that this so-called "understanding" was not enough. If results were to improve, so must communication.

The job description can be used to communicate standards in a variety of ways. It can be done by referring to operating manuals, guidelines, procedures or the like. This would keep the length of the job description down and does save repetition, but it may involve job holders in a great deal of complicated cross-referencing. It also relies on the references concerned being completely up to date.

It can also be done by incorporating standards into the description of duties as shown in the previous example relating to the manager's responsibility for motivating staff. An alternative is to add a standards column to the job description. Once again, take the insurance claims clerk example:

Key area	Duties	Standard of Performance
Ensure that all departmental filing, etc...	File all new claims, etc...	Standard of performance is reached when: 90% of new claims are filed daily; completed claims are removed and archived within four working days of being settled; alphabetical and numerical ordering is 95% accurate when checked quarterly by supervisor.

This is clear enough, but such detail is going to create a long and directive job description which may not encourage flexibility, growth or initiative.

One method of stating standards of performance is to set "negative" measurements (eg "No more than four mistakes per month in outgoing correspondence"). This is clear and allows for human fallibility. It also gives the job holder scope to exceed the standard. However, the example of the secretary who always made four mistakes because she was permitted to, demonstrates the "self-fulfilling prophecy" problem of this approach.

All methods have their pros and cons. Whatever format is used, it must be the one that managers and staff feel is the most helpful to them in doing their jobs and achieving results.

Access to Job Descriptions

A survey amongst a selection of typical employees would probably show that they do not have copies of their job descriptions, that they had one and lost it, or that they have one to hand but never refer to it. Managers must ensure that their staff always have an up-to-date copy of their job description. Whether these staff choose to use it is a matter for them to decide, but encouragement to do so is part of the communication process.

Access to, understanding of, and consultation in the construction of, thoughtfully prepared job descriptions and clearly defined standards of performance, is the first and most fundamental of the steps leading to effective performance appraisal.

Chapter 3
Preparing for the Appraisal Meeting

A good performance appraisal interview is as much a preparation skill as a communication skill. Most managers, by the very nature of their jobs, are used to planning and organising. Many of them, however, would say that they are not comfortable with the idea of the "eyeball to eyeball" type of communication required in an appraisal interview. Once it is understood that thorough preparation is the key to handling the face-to-face encounter confidence soon grows to develop the interpersonal skills required to carry out an effective performance appraisal interview.

Preparing the Appraisee

Appraisees should always have approximately 10–14 days' notice that their appraisal interview is due. If the appraisal round is carried out at the same time of year for everyone in the organisation, a team meeting at which all members of staff are reminded about objectives and what is involved may have been held. Even so, each individual should have his or her own personal reminder, not only about the date and time but about the nature of the whole exercise.

The reminder could be a brief verbal one, but a preparation for appraisal form is particularly useful in helping appraisees get used to the idea that they are going to have the opportunity to discuss aspects of their jobs in a positive and constructive way. It is not unusual for appraisees to be very restrained in answering some of the questions posed by the preparation form if they have to return it. Questions about aspirations and interests may be answered somewhat politically or the self-assessment may be painfully self-effacing. Therefore the use of a preparation form should be viewed with this constraint in mind, and whether it is returned so that the manager can use it in preparing for the interview is a matter for individuals to decide as appropriate. It is worth pointing out, however, that if appraisees are going to hand over their thoughts before the meeting they would have every right to ask to see their manager's preparation beforehand! Whatever decision is made about returning preparation forms, appraisees should be confident that their preparation is not a waste of time and that it will form a significant part of the appraisal meeting.

Appraisees may be asked to ensure that, if necessary, their duties will be covered while they are at their appraisal meeting, although more often than not the manager will see to such a detail. Who arranges the necessary cover is not important — what matters is that appraisers and appraisees do not rush the meeting because of pressing operational needs.

Practical Preparation

Ensuring Privacy

Appraisal interviews must take place in private without any interruption, except in dire circumstances. If managers have their own offices this is not a problem. If the appraisee has an office it may even be appropriate to use that. However, the trend towards open planning in offices can mean that private places are hard to find. Even offices with huge viewing windows are a problem (nothing can be heard but interpreting facial expressions and gestures can be an interesting pastime for those on the other side of the window). It is possibly not wise to take appraisees to rooms which they would otherwise never see the inside of to carry out interviews. A catering company often used its plush boardroom; many employees confessed to finding this an intimidating environment.

Whatever the problems, they must be overcome to ensure that the appraisal interview can be carried out in a private and relaxed atmosphere. Having a co-ordinator book out interview rooms, taking hotel accommodation or using local commercial facilities are some of the options which might be considered if managers cannot easily find a suitable room.

Room Layout

The layout of the interview room is a matter of personal preference. A familiar office should not look very different from usual. People become comfortable with certain settings and the sudden appearance of a coffee table and two easy chairs could actually make an appraisee suspicious.

Chairs placed on opposite sides of a desk may create a confrontational atmosphere, although a desk is considerably more useful than a coffee table, bearing in mind the various items of paperwork likely to be used during the encounter. A practical layout is to place comfortable chairs at right angles to one another at a desk which is clear of everything except items relevant to the appraisal interview.

There is no ideal layout for an interview room — a setting in which both parties are physically and psychologically comfortable should be the main aim.

Timing

"How long should I allow for the interview?" is a question many managers will ask. The quality of the interview should not be judged by the length of time it takes, although an extremely short one could leave both parties wondering if they really had had a worthwhile discussion. Equally, an extremely long interview could indicate poor planning, a lot of repetition and some pointless haggling.

The safest option is probably to time an appraisal interview to start as soon as the morning or post-lunchtime routines have been cleared away so that it will not be rushed with breaks or hometime in mind. It is also prudent not to arrange too many interviews in one day. Rushing one interview in order to start the next one on time is not helpful. Appraisal is sufficiently demanding to say that one or two a day is as much as most managers can cope with.

The Manager's Review

By far the largest task in preparing for appraisal is the manager's consideration of the whole review period. Performance against the set standards and agreed objectives has to be assessed, action plans to assist in future improvement and development have to be considered, other people may need to be consulted, some research may have to be done, and an interview plan or agenda will have to be drawn up.

Assessing Performance

Considering how appraisees have matched up to the key areas and standards as stated in their job descriptions or to the objectives which have been agreed with them is as good a place as any to start preparing for an appraisal interview. Appraisal is meant to be a continuous process and the appraisal interview should be a summary of the work of the previous review period. However, the human mind naturally focuses on recent events, so great care has to be taken to review the whole period and not just the immediate past.

Some things will have been performed extremely well, others satisfactorily, and others well below standard. Whatever assessments the appraiser makes at this stage, it must be borne in mind that until the interview has taken place and the appraisee's views are heard, the assessment is incomplete. Establishing the facts of the matter by the use of examples is essential, although producing some to emphasise the stronger areas is just as important as using them to demonstrate that certain things need improving.

There are always reasons for the performance levels employees achieve. At the preparatory stage these can be thought out, given that this can only be guesswork until the appraisal interview has taken place. The impact of the various elements of the job have to be put into context too. Some things are just not worth the expenditure of effort required to change them, whilst others certainly are. Establishing the reasons for good performance can give a much clearer insight into an employee's particular talents, potential and ambitions. It can also be extremely useful in establishing why certain other areas of performance are not so good and how the matter of raising standards might be addressed. Additionally, only when the real reasons for poor performance are uncovered and understood can any attempt be made to agree what action is required to ensure that standards will improve.

Possible reasons for good performance

(a) Enjoying the particular task or having a specific aptitude for it.
(b) Commitment to the task which has been achieved through consultation and communication with the individual.

(c) Good availability of resources.

(d) Excellent training in the task.

(e) An element of competition which spurs the individual on.

(f) Growth in the individual which has released hitherto unrealised potential.

(g) A desire to "get on", whether this is in the existing job or whether it is sheer ambition.

(h) It could be worth thinking through the possibility that the standard has been consistently met because it is too low.

Whilst considering the reasons for good performance, the pitfall of the "halo" effect might be examined. Some employees are good at certain aspects of their job which are particularly "visible" and important. Some may have done so well recently that previous problems have been overlooked. Some are good at aspects which their managers value highly. Some are good at "politically" important parts of their job. Some have been historically very good and recent changes for the worst have not been noticed. Some are simply perceived, somewhat subjectively, as being "good eggs" particularly by managers who tend to like people who are rather like themselves. In all these cases it is important not to let the positive aspects obscure the areas where there are problems, and where improvements could be made.

The accounts manager who felt that he should "go easy" on one of his representatives at their appraisal meeting provides an excellent example of this "syndrome". The salesman concerned always overspent his entertainment budget, frequently could not be tracked down and his administrative duties were carried out abysmally. However, he was making record sales in difficult times and the more negative aspects of his performance were glossed over at his appraisal. He therefore continued to overspend his budgets, go missing and send in illegible reports and orders. Ultimately his good sales were negated by his large expenses and the number of incorrect orders which had to be returned and reissued.

Possible reasons for poor performance

(a) The task concerned is disliked by the individual or he or she has no aptitude for it. If the task is a particularly important part of the whole job, the person's suitability for the post should be reviewed.

(b) There is no commitment to the task because it has been arbitrarily imposed and its relevance is not understood. The task may not have been adequately explained in the first instance, perhaps in the job description.

(c) Resources are lacking or other elements out of the appraisee's control are creating obstacles.

(d) Training and follow-up has been inadequate or the individual has found it difficult to take the task on in spite of adequate training and information about what is involved.

(e) Lack of confidence to do the task or to admit that he or she is unable to do it and therefore ask for help.

(f) Physical or emotional problems, or a general diminishment in potential for other reasons.

(g) The processes involved in the task could be difficult and outmoded and need examining.

(h) The standard imposed could be unrealistically high.

(i) Lack of practice in an infrequently performed task or sheer boredom in a task which is all too frequently called for.

(j) The unfortunate perception that if one is good at something, the reward is getting more of it to do. (Or indeed, if one is bad at something the job will be given to someone else to do!)

(k) Insufficient monitoring, feedback and action has taken place about the task as it is performed on a day-to-day basis.

Clearly the matter of considering poor performance is more complex. Often the apparent reason is not the real one. A manager was criticised for the quality of the departmental reports she was sending in at the end of each quarter. A report writing course was considered to be the answer to the problem, and the manager was duly dispatched on one. At the end of the next quarter the report she sent in was no improvement on her previous attempts. Further examination of the matter revealed that the manager was quite capable of constructing a report. The content was the problem and this was because she had no idea what the report was for, who read it, how the information was used and how it fitted into the management processes of her company. A couple of days spent on secondment to the various "users" of the information brought about the necessary improvement.

In considering poor performance, there is the opposite of the "halo" effect — the "horns" effect. Certain hapless individuals, in spite of whatever attempts they make, are never perceived to improve because they cannot shake off a poor image. There are others who generally have a good performance record but recent problems have obscured their more normal behaviour. Some people are good at most aspects of their job, but happen to have particular problems with a rather political or visible aspect of it, which tends to obliterate their otherwise good performance. Frequently, this sort of issue tends to stick for longer than it should when a person has been associated with a notorious mistake or failure. Potentially they may never recover from such an incident. Of course there are also those who just do not fit in, particularly those who are so different from their managers that they are judged subjectively and unfairly on a benchmark which is based only on the manager's likes and dislikes, and definitely not on organisational norms.

The "horns" effect is more dangerous than the "halo" effect since its negative repercussions will almost automatically be labelled unfair and bring the appraisal process into disrepute very quickly.

Talking to Others

When preparing an assessment of performance, managers may often feel that other people will need to be consulted. The individual's peer group would of course not be the right people to talk to, and talking to customers or outside agencies could produce some subjective and ill-informed judgments.

However, talking to senior people who are involved with the appraisee is all part of preparation. It would be important, for example, for a personnel manager to talk to other senior managers about how a personnel assistant has carried out a recruitment project with them. It would be necessary for an administration manager to discuss with the various other managers in the organisation how the secretaries allocated to them have performed.

Feedback from the right people is a vital part of preparing for appraisal, although the appraising manager must always be satisfied of the truth, relevance, validity and objectivity of the information received. Anything less would be unfair to the appraisee and do nothing for the manager's own credibility in the appraisal situation.

Getting Documentation Together

Effective performance appraisal cannot be carried out without certain items of documentation to hand. Some examples of these might be:

(a) job descriptions

(b) previous appraisals and targets

(c) personal files containing details of relevant incidents during the review period

(d) appraisal report forms, as yet blank (these are *not* filled in until the interview is complete — the appraisal outcome will be seen to be a foregone conclusion if the form has been filled in to any degree beforehand)

(e) any documentation needed to support factual examples

(f) the employee's preparation form if it has been returned

(g) rating or salary scales if these are relevant to the exercise.

The Interview Plan

An interview plan or agenda is essential to ensure that everything is fully discussed at the appraisal meeting. Some managers like to determine in what order discussion points will take place and there are a number of options in how the order can be decided. The simplest is to go through the key areas of the job description in the order in which they are written, and then work through the various other prompts such as training requirements or development plans which the appraisal form offers. The manager refers to the notes prepared beforehand about each heading, and guides the discussion through to its conclusion.

It may be preferable to be a little more selective about what the discussion starts and ends with. Beginning with something about which very positive feedback can be given will get the encounter off to a much better start. Similarly, keeping something positive so that the interview can be ended on a high note is desirable, although of course a summary of the action plan agreed is a useful way to conclude, and by its very nature an action plan must be positive. The disadvantage of this more selective approach is that appraisees may feel that they have been patronised at the start of their interview in preparation for the less pleasant points to come.

Some managers use the "slicing" method, which is to deal with good and bad items alternately. However, it is unlikely that areas of discussion will fall so neatly into place and it is easy to imagine an appraisee paying little attention to some positive feedback, knowing that it heralds the next, less positive discussion topic.

Perhaps the most effective method of setting the agenda is to ask appraisees how they would like to proceed. Taking a few moments at the beginning of the interview to give a résumé of what needs to be covered, asking if the appraisee has any additional points, and then working out the batting order, is worthwhile. This does not mean that the manager's plan is dismissed; indeed the plan is even more important as a checklist that everything which needs to be discussed is fully covered.

A good agenda should also minimise the use of an "additional comments" or "any other business" section of the appraisal report form. Often, such sections are filled in with unnecessary and trite remarks which add nothing to the quality of the appraisal report. A good business meeting agenda only has an "any other business" section as an emergency or courtesy measure. A good appraisal agenda should follow the same principle.

The phrase "to fail to prepare is to prepare to fail" may be somewhat overused but nowhere is it more true than in the arena of appraisal interviewing. Good preparation, preferably by both appraisers and appraisees, is the second of the steps in carrying out effective performance appraisal.

Chapter 4
Conducting Appraisal Interviews

The objective of an appraisal interview is to research and plan ahead for mutual gain. Seeing employees every day does not dispense with the need for providing an opportunity for good quality communication with them. The appraisal meeting will probably be easier where good ongoing communication is the norm; for those managers who are more remote from their staff for various operational or geographical reasons, the appraisal interview has even more relevance and validity as a management tool.

The Joint Approach

What sets an appraisal apart from most other types of interview is that it should adopt the "joint approach". This is also a technique used in counselling and appraisal interviews are often seen as counselling to improve performance.

The joint approach is based on the idea that confrontation about shortcomings in performance and the imposition of solutions to them are not going to get the commitment required from employees to make improvements. Managers have to see themselves not as "judge and jury" in the appraisal situation, but as "enablers". The joint approach employs a discussion technique which is designed to avoid patronising appraisees or confronting them about their strengths and weaknesses. It is about developing awareness and gaining agreement to plans for development or improvement.

To some degree, the boss/subordinate relationship should be sublimated in order to get down to the absolute truth and to agree the way ahead. It would be unwise to sublimate it too much however, since there may be times when all the patience in the world does not reap its reward. The appraisee may refuse to face up to problem areas and finally has to be told that current levels of performance are not acceptable and must be improved. Even when this last line of defence has had to be used, however, solutions should not initially be imposed. The joint approach should be used again to identify and agree the way forward.

The following extract demonstrates the technique in a situation where an appraisee has a problem in the supervision of a small office. All the staff have to deal frequently with queries about customers' orders over the telephone or by letter. The appraising manager is not altogether happy about the image being projected by the department's telephone manner or style of letter writing. It has already been discussed but somewhat overtaken by other departmental priorities, so nothing has been done about it to date.

(Question types are denoted for reference in the later section on questioning techniques.)

Appraiser: So the next item on the agenda we agreed is the department's handling of customer queries and complaints. (Statement)

Appraisee: Fine.

Appraiser: We have discussed this before haven't we? (Questioning statement) How do you feel about it at the moment? (Open question)

Appraisee: It's OK, I can't see how it could be any different. We answer the phone as best we can with all the pressure we are under, and we have a few standard letters that we can just push out if orders are late in being dispatched.

Appraiser: How do you feel that you should be dealt with on the telephone when you are a customer — say when you are ringing up the gas company or the washing machine service agents? (Open question)

Appraisee: I expect politeness, to have my problems understood and not to be treated as if they were unimportant, and to get some action.

Appraiser: How do you go about listening to your staff dealing with customers over the phone? (Open question)

Appraisee: I can't say that I ever do, but I have some idea about the standard because we all work in one office.

Appraiser: How do you think customers are being treated? (Open question)

Appraisee: Now you mention it, probably not as well as they might be. We all tend to fob people off because we are under pressure and then of course, they only ring back again another time.

Appraiser: They get annoyed about that don't they? Remember we discussed that complaint which came to me from the chap who said he was passed round from pillar to post, and still never got his order filled? (Closed question) What do you think happened there? (Open question)

Appraisee: As I said at the time, we were snowed under that morning and he caught us at a bad time. It was such a small order, particularly from him, because he's a regular and usually has much larger quantities.

Appraiser: You've hit the nail right on the head there. We just couldn't afford to lose the likes of him. (Statement) So what do you think the answer is to avoid a repetition of that incident? (Open question) (Long pause — interviewer waits for response)

Appraisee: Well, I'd better see the people concerned again and tell them that it just won't do and it is not to happen again.

Appraiser: How do you think that that will change things? (Open question)

Appraisee: What do you mean?

Appraiser: Do you think that a rollicking will equip everyone to do the job better in future? (Probing closed question)

Appraisee: Put like that, no I don't suppose it would.

Appraiser: You don't think it would? (Rebound question) (Long pause — interviewer waits for response)

Appraisee: Well, we need to get better organised so that customers ringing up aren't treated as a nuisance. We couldn't do without them could we?

Appraiser: How easily could that be done? (Open question)

Appraisee: Well, one of my targets so far is to streamline office procedures. Perhaps I could actually have a phone rota so that everyone isn't disturbed all the time. If they are on phone duty they can be doing less difficult tasks in between calls.

Appraiser: Would that be wasteful? Does the phone ring that much? (Closed probing question)

Appraisee: Oh yes. We probably spend about three hours daily between us on the phone dealing with routine dispatches or queries.

Appraiser: I'm not too sure about this. Could you get a duty rota up for me to look at? (Closed question)

Appraisee: No problem.

Appraiser: By when? (Specific question)

Appraisee: Beginning of next month.

Appraiser: I'd prefer it sooner. (Statement)

Appraisee: No can do — I'm on holiday next week, and I can't do it before I go; I'm just too busy with the interim stock figures.

Appraiser: How about the end of the week after next? (Specific question)

Appraisee: Yes — let me note that down. If it's OK we'll implement it by the first of next month.

Appraiser: Yes — I'll note it down too. Now, about the actual telephone handling. What can we do about that? (Open question)

Appraisee: Could you see the training officer about it? There are some courses for it I know, because someone in accounts went on one.

Appraiser: I'd like you to consider what you would want from the course first. They are good but expensive. (Statement) If we could clear the cost, who would you like to go on it? (Hypothetical open question)

Appraisee: All of us ideally. Would that be possible? If not, just me, and I can do some training for the others. We ought to have a consistent standard for all of us I think, so I could draw up a checklist for us to use after the course.

Appraiser: If you could jot down some of your ideas about what you would want from the course, and then go and see John in Training, we could get this thing going fairly soon I think. (Statement)

Appraisee: I'll let you have a copy of what I put together after my holiday.

Appraiser: Well you've got the rota to do by then haven't you? If I just say that I expect you to come back to me with it within six weeks having cleared costs and got at least yourself on some sort of telephone handling course that will do nicely. Could we discuss the others attending then, when we know a bit more about what's on offer and what we can afford? I'll let John know that you're coming up to see him.

So let's get that all noted down. You are going to try to achieve a consistently higher standard of handling customer queries on the telephone in the department. How would you go about actually getting that standard clear? (Open question)

Appraisee: That business about how I would like to be treated gives me some ideas about how I might write it down.

Appraiser: That's a good idea. (Statement)

Appraiser: To achieve this standard you are going to produce a duty rota for me to OK, which will allow the staff to give more attention to dealing with telephone calls. I'll have that by the sixteenth of the month and if it's all right, you'll start using it by the first of next month.

You are also going to come back to me in six weeks' time (I'll work the date out later when I write this all up properly) with at least yourself booked on a telephone handling course, if it is possible. Whoever ends up on the course, you are still going to produce a departmental standard related to the practices suggested on it. (Summary) How long after the course do you think you need to do that? (Specific question)

Appraisee: Oh, I'll do that within a week — better to strike while I'm still keen!

Appraiser: Right, well I've got all that down. Now, about these standard letters. I'm sure I've got a few around here somewhere ... (Statement)

106

The chances are that this appraisee will achieve these things and create lasting improvements. There has been no confrontation and no imposition, but nothing has been left unattended to. Some rather "hard line" managers often ask why they cannot just go straight to the point, without "beating around the bush". The answer is that by encouraging people to identify and discuss problems, and to formulate the answers to them, they are much more likely to be motivated to do something about them. If the hardliners want to go straight to the point, they may do so, but they are less likely to see real and *lasting* improvement accrue from their appraisal meetings.

Other Interviewing Skills

Opening and Creating Rapport

The opening phases of an appraisal interview are clearly going to be very important in determining the atmosphere which will prevail throughout the meeting. Putting people at their ease is a necessary opening skill, so that they will feel comfortable enough to enter into an honest and productive discussion.

Sometimes it is necessary for both parties to clarify their relationship in the context of appraisal. In some instances where managers are normally rather formal they may wish to encourage a more informal atmosphere. In certain other instances, managers who are normally rather "chummy" with subordinates may wish to distance themselves a little.

A comfortable and preferably familiar room layout is important, and offering refreshment is a worthwhile gesture as long as it is not totally out of character with the manager's usual style. Offering coffee and cigarettes to appraisees is likely to cause some suspicion if such a welcome is not normal in the manager's office!

Trite remarks about the weather, health, etc, are not helpful with most appraisees; they can usually see that these are stock preliminaries and would prefer the courtesy of getting down to business quickly. It is not appropriate to begin with remarks about the exercise being over soon since this indicates a lack of commitment.

An initial reminder from the manager about the purpose of performance appraisal and the appraisal interview is important. At this point some discussion can take place on the structure of the meeting and the order of play can be decided between the participants. Explaining that notes will be taken so that the manager can write up an accurate record of the interview is a courtesy, as is offering appraisees a note pad and pen if they have forgotten their own.

The first stages of the appraisal interview should be thought out carefully, so as to reduce any apprehension, suspicion or nervousness, perhaps felt by both sides. A great deal of the potential for apprehension about the event can be removed during the preparatory stages. Communicating with the appraisee about what to expect, and thorough planning by the appraiser are vital elements in creating the right climate for the appraisal meeting. A few well-chosen words and gestures to get the meeting on its way are worth some consideration beforehand.

Questioning

Since the main objective of an appraisal interview is to get people talking and to find out their views on matters, the appraising manager needs to consider how best to construct questions and statements to keep the discussion moving and relevant.

Open questions, beginning with who, what, why, where, how or when are useful in getting people to talk and open up. Too much use of them, however, will make the interviewer sound more like an interrogator. It should also be noted that open questions can elicit some rather open answers, and at some stage specific or closed questions are necessary to obtain certain facts and to keep the conversation relevant. Hypothetical questions, which offer possible solutions, can be used to test reactions and the validity of feedback.

Rebound questions, which simply repeat the last part of the appraisee's response, are very useful for those who are less forthcoming and are also helpful in probing more deeply when necessary.

The use of silence is something which appraisers should practice. The temptation to answer their own questions or put words into appraisees' mouths is almost too much for some managers. It follows that if the interviewer does not keep quiet occasionally, the interviewee will not be able to speak up and achieve the desired ratio of talking, which should be about 30 per cent appraiser and 70 per cent appraisee.

All the types of question mentioned above have their rightful place in appraisal interviewing, but none is virtuous if used in excess. Moderation in use is the secret of a balanced interview. The various types of question have been noted in the transcript on pages 104-6 to illustrate how they might be used effectively.

Listening Skills

All the careful questioning in the world will not be of any use at all if appraisers do not listen to the answers. Just as important as asking the right questions is demonstrating that the answers are being listened to.

Maintaining eye contact, nodding, gesturing and keeping an "open" posture are all physical indicators that listening is taking place. The proof of real listening, however, is in the interviewer's responses, in that questions should be obviously linked to the appraisee's answers. Listening is also demonstrated when notes are made of the salient points. The best test of listening comes when the manager summarises; if listening and understanding has taken place, the summary will be an accurate one.

Keeping Control

Dealing with the talkative

The talkative appraisee may be interesting but inclined to go off at irrelevant tangents. To control a situation like this the interviewer can blatantly interrupt to get the interview back on the track, or perhaps try a summary of the important points so far, so that it is clear that enough has been said. Changing the pace of the interview by using more closed and specific questions for a while might be advisable in a case like this one.

Getting people to open up

Not getting someone to open up is a less obvious form of losing interview control. To some degree the interviewee has control here, for often it is he or she who has decided that they will not assist in achieving a productive outcome.

Plenty of open or rebound questions may get some response from the less talkative subject. The use of periods of silence by the interviewer may be difficult, but worth a try.

However, the real issue here is *why* the appraisee does not want to open up. Is it mistrust of appraisal in general or of the appraiser? Is it a failure to comprehend the relevance of the exercise? Is it a crippling lack of communication skill? Is it a fear of confrontation or criticism? Is it a desire not to co-operate, which is typical of the individual anyway?

If the interviewer's technique cannot get appraisees to open up, then all that is left is to confront their lack of participation in the meeting. This could even result in the interview being abandoned and rescheduled. At the very worst, it might even mean giving up altogether for the time being. Some employees seem to want this outcome and it might be the best way to deal with the situation if an acceptable standard of performance in the job is being reached. The appraisal report should record an agreement about what course of action is decided upon and it remains for the manager to monitor the individual very carefully in the succeeding months.

Drifting into other types of interview

The opportunity for a private discussion with their manager may encourage some appraisees to offload about other things which are currently affecting them. Ideally, the appraisal interview should remain faithful to its original objectives, but there are times when it becomes impossible to ignore the fact that things are not working quite to plan.

If the appraisee becomes upset because personal problems come to light, it might be as well to say that the appraisal can be done at another time and continue with a counselling session. It should be noted that employees with serious performance problems may well try to avoid being held accountable for them, by producing some sort of mitigating "disability". That is, when the reasons for poor performance are being discussed, it may seem a reasonable way out for them to suggest that domestic or health problems are to blame.

Employees who wish to introduce or chew over matters relating to discipline and grievances should be reminded about the parameters of the appraisal interview and encouraged to make an alternative appointment to discuss these other issues. If they persist, then perhaps it would be as well to abandon the meeting altogether and make other arrangements for both the appraisal and the discipline or grievance issue.

Over-compliance

Some appraisees will, for reasons best known to themselves, approach appraisal with an over-compliant attitude. They will agree to everything, accept any extra objectives and take on board any praise or criticism which is levelled at them.

It is possible that this attitude is taken by the appraisee to be the one that confirms that he or she is an exemplary employee. However, it may be designed to avoid too much probing. Whatever the reason, the appraiser needs to investigate it and make it abundantly clear that the purpose of the appraisal meeting is to communicate honestly so that improvements can take place for the benefit of all. Feedback, negative or positive, is required from the appraisee so that this objective can be reached, and this must be emphasised and understood.

Disagreement, confrontation, arguing

Certain appraisers and appraisees dislike confrontation and will often view the appraisal meeting as providing too good an opportunity for it. A desire to avoid confrontation may lead to managers being too lenient or appraisees too compliant. Most managers at some time in their career as appraisers, will have to deal with confrontation, but if an appraisal interview degenerates into something of a showdown, it can demonstrate a regrettable lack of skill on the part of the appraiser. However, appraisal is essentially a very "human" business and occasional confrontation is almost inevitable.

Dealing with heated emotions and confrontation is a matter of stopping the proceedings before they get out of control. There is no point in carrying on a discussion in which the parties are unlikely to reach agreement. Steering the conversation back to an even pitch and trying to salvage a positive conclusion is vital. If agreement cannot be reached, then at least a failure to agree can be recorded. Perhaps the matter can be discussed at another time when both sides have had time to consider it. If things really get serious, the appraisee can be invited to use the appeals procedure, and talk the issue through with a higher authority. Either way, this must be noted and conscientiously followed through.

In reflecting on the confrontation, managers must consider the reasons for it having happened. One of the most common causes is that managers fail to recognise outside influences or lack of resources beyond the job holder's control which are to blame for problems in performance. Another common reason is the natural human resistance to any type of criticism however carefully it is levelled. Often managers get into confrontational situations because they dislike any sort of challenge to their own authority or they cannot handle implied criticisms about their managerial ability.

It cannot be overlooked that confrontation may take place because the appraiser and appraisee simply do not like each other. Most managers will have to appraise someone they do not particularly like personally. Personal likes and dislikes are likely to influence management/staff relations in some way, however wrong this may be. This situation serves to emphasise how important it is to keep appraisal entirely objective, factual, fair and positive. It is not beyond the bounds of possibility that where personal likes and dislikes are concerned, allegations of discriminatory treatment may even be made. Again, managers have to rise above their personal considerations, even if appraisees choose not to rise above theirs, and conduct their appraisals in an entirely professional and impartial manner.

The actual method and style of the appraisal scheme itself may be to blame for some elements of confrontation. Where money is a factor, where qualities are assessed or where grades are rather arbitrarily awarded, confrontation is more likely to occur. Again, the point is made, that nothing should be decided in advance, the appraisal meeting should be geared towards an objective discussion of performance and future plans, and the appraisal report should be seen as an honest and accurate record of the discussion.

Summaries

Making summaries as the appraisal meeting develops is a useful way of structuring the interview and indicating its progress. It is also extremely valid in terms of checking understanding since the summary will form the basis of what eventually goes into the appraisal report form, and it is going to be an advantage to clear up any misunderstandings about feedback during the interview itself. To write up the appraisal report form incorrectly means troublesome re-writes, but it may also cause a degree of disappointment or suspicion on the part of the appraisee.

A final summary at the close of the appraisal should be formulated in order to assess whether or not the meeting's objectives have been achieved and it can be satisfactorily concluded. This summary can be difficult to do well because it may be involved. It may be necessary for a summarisation to take place at a later meeting, when the report form has been completed, can be read through and the various copies signed. Some managers prefer to write up the report of the interview at the end of the meeting. This certainly is more convenient, but does not offer any opportunity for reflection or any necessary research. The skill in writing this record of the assessment of performance and the plans made lies only in using simple and accurate terms which anyone who has to use the report will clearly understand. The appraisee signs the report form, not to agree or disagree with any assessments or action plans contained within it. Discussion on those subjects has taken place within the interview and is noted down accordingly. The signature is to indicate that the appraisal report form is a true and fully understood account of what was included at the appraisal meeting and that its content has been agreed.

Competence in appraisal interviewing does take practice and only improves with honest commitment to learning from experience. The appraisal interview is the single most important event in the whole process as far as the appraisee is concerned and it is vital that this third step in effective performance appraisal is carried out with genuine concern for the impact that it is likely to have. Confidence and skill are necessary to re-assure appraisees that the appraisal meeting is indeed a worthwhile exercise.

Chapter 5
Agreeing Action Plans

The action which will result from an appraisal interview will fall broadly into three categories:

(a) training or remedial action in order to bring weaker areas up to standard
(b) further training, coaching or planned experience to develop satisfactory or stronger areas and to broaden experience (possibly with advancement in mind) and
(c) targets or objectives (words which mean the same thing in this context) to give the appraisee some goals to work towards in the following months.

Some schemes will separate the first two categories from the third; others will combine all plans into a set of defined aims for the appraisee. For the purpose of this discussion the term "action" will be used to include all three categories.

Whatever method is used there are some simple rules for managers to use so that their own and their employee's efforts are not wasted by misunderstanding and lack of commitment.

The most important feature of a successful action plan is that it has been agreed. People can often discipline themselves far more rigorously than might be expected, and to agree action may actually be to stretch employees beyond the manager's original and more conservative aims.

Action should not be distributed clinically throughout each key area or item of the job description; it should only be planned where absolutely

relevant and where improvements can be perceived to be mutually beneficial.

It hardly seems necessary to add that all planned actions must be
achievable in some degree, and that all influences must be thought
through as a part of the action planning process. Any expected changes
within the organisation must of course be considered. There would be
very little credibility attached to an action plan which had not taken into
account an impending restructuring or relocation. Part of the manager's
follow-up of agreed action must be a careful monitoring of changes or de-
velopments which may affect employees' chances of successfully completing their action plans.

The appraisee should be clear about what any planned action is trying
to achieve. It should not necessarily be seen as extra work to do (although
this may be the case). Rather, it is a matter of raising standards and developing ability through the careful planning of training and task allocation.

The relevance of any planned action must be identifiable. It must be
obvious how the action will make a difference to the appraisee's performance or potential. It would be very easy, for example, to send well-
rounded performers off to research something which they are unlikely to
find beneficial simply so that they can be given a target of some sort.

Planning action for some employees may not always seem appropriate
if they are perfectly contented and have no need or desire to develop further. However, some action to add interest to the job might legitimately be
agreed (becoming a mentor for new staff, for example). Sending a pro-
spective retiree on a retirement seminar would constitute a *bona fide* action
plan.

Action plans need to be agreed with the appraisee's development and
effectiveness in mind as a priority, but it would be quite inappropriate to
set targets which have no bearing on departmental or organisational objectives, needs and standards. To send an employee on a desk top publish-
ing course because it is a natural progression in his or her word processing
skills is hardly worthwhile if the organisation has no plans to invest in a
DTP package. To agree an improvement in the daily sales call rate from
55 to 60 with a telesales representative, to bring it up to the normal standard would seem sensible and reasonable. To ask him or her to increase it
within six months to 65 might be consistent with a sales drive. To ask a
good performer to increase to 70 when there are no resources to meet the
extra sales for the time being would be ill considered. The fact that good
performance is often rewarded with more of the same is a factor to bear in
mind here too. In such a case, an objective to develop the dimensions of

the job might be preferable (eg to prepare a new recording procedure to ensure that customers are not called twice by different departments).

NB An exception to the relevance to organisational needs rule, may be found in some professions, eg a nurse in training may need experience in certain types of child care to complete a phase of development. This particular facility may not be available or necessary in the current appointment, so in this case an external attachment may be needed to fulfil the training provider's obligation to the profession — to produce a comprehensively trained nurse.

Action plans must be specifically outlined and the standards required made absolutely clear, perhaps by referring to established policies or procedures as a control. Giving a definite time frame is necessary to give structure and impact, and the limits of authority should be stated.

The following examples may seem a little prescriptive for some tastes, but they do serve to illustrate the point. Remember, too, that these details will have been at least agreed with, and possibly even suggested by, the appraisee.

(a) Rather than "understand customer service better", try "attend the meeting of customer service committee on 20 May to inform it about current departmental efforts to improve service, and to formulate future initiatives in line with the 'Customer Service Policy', for discussion with and approval by me by 30 May. After consultation with departmental staff, prepare for implementation by end of June".

(b) Rather than "reduce wastage in department", try "prepare proposals to bring weekly departmental wastage figures down to 1.9 per cent by year end, for me by 10 June. All proposals to be in line with Health and Safety procedures, and consistent with minimum quality requirements stated in the product manuals. On approval by Division Director, plan to implement proposals to bring figures down to 2.9 per cent by 30 September, and 1.9 per cent by 31 December".

Action plans should also be measurable. Were further initiatives for improving customer service in the department formulated and eventually implemented within company guidelines by the due date, or were they not? Were the weekly departmental wastage figures brought down to 1.9 per cent by the year end within acceptable limits of safety and quality, or were they not? With this in mind, it is useful to concentrate more on outcomes than input, when agreeing action plans. An employee may be sent on a course to develop his or her staff training ability. This input will form the first part of the action plan. More important, however, is what can be achieved as a result of attending the course. The rest of the plan should focus on planning, carrying out and evaluating tasks which will demonstrate the worth of the training (ie outcomes, not input).

Clearly the dates for the various action points should be carefully spaced out to avoid undue pressure at any one time, or a possible anticlimax when everything has come to the boil together and then "gone cold". Action which is set over a longer period needs a number of review points built in so that the project is carried out in reasonable stages and not rushed at shortly before the date for completion. This also offers an opportunity for a further demonstration of constructive support from the manager. If the appraisal review period is as long as a year, it is advisable to review the total action plan after approximately six months and agree some further objectives until the next formal appraisal. These may serve to stretch appraisees further, encourage, or merely interest them. However, all the same rules of planning action will apply even at an interim review.

A certain amount of variation in the degree of difficulty is always required in planning action points. Some items which can be achieved more easily and motivate the employee into further achievement are worthwhile. Equally, some items which will challenge and stretch (as opposed to overload) the individual need to be included to extend his or her development.

Particular care must be taken if plans involve others — a supervisor may train staff very well in a new system but could hardly be held accountable if one member of the team is unable to take on new ideas.

As with the writing of job descriptions, how much detail action plans are recorded in and how prescriptive they are, is very much a matter of organisational choice. Some plans or people may require close monitoring. Other situations can allow for a great deal of latitude in how goals are ultimately reached. There should be some consistency at the various levels of the organisation, and most certainly within departments. However, the essential principles remain the same — action plans at this fourth stage of implementing effective performance appraisal must be:

(a) agreed
(b) distributed carefully in relation to job content
(c) achievable having considered likely external influences

(d) clear in intent
(e) relevant
(f) appropriate
(g) related to organisational as well as appraisees' needs
(h) specifically outlined, with clear standards, controls, time frames, and limits of authority
(i) carefully spaced out and monitored
(j) varied in the degree of challenge offered.

The following is a further illustration (page 120) of a form designed to summarise action plans and serve as a working document for appraisers and appraisees. It has been partially completed to emphasise further the main principles highlighted in the previous section.

(In this particular example, an office services supervisor has agreed that there has not been cover provided for the switchboard according to the standard specified in the job description. Note how the action plans are linked to those of the staff in the department — candidates for training will be sought when their appraisals are completed. An objective has also been agreed to reduce photocopying costs which is part of the whole company's "good housekeeping" drive.)

CONFIDENTIAL
ACTION PLAN FOR: J. SMITH 24th September

Details of planned action.	Standard of performance to be achieved. Controls to be used.	Date by which target to be achieved.	Interim or follow-up action required.
To arrange and carry out switch-board train-ing for two additional members of staff, so as to provide adequate cover for switchboard duties.	Full training in switch-board duties to be arranged with training department. Members of staff to be able to operate switch-board according to instruction manual. Full cover for switch-board to be main-tained at all times as per job description.	Both members of staff to be available for switchboard relief by 31 January.	Select staff to be trained following their appraisals by 9 October. Arrange train-ing with train-ing department by 1 December and commence practical train-ing by 14 December.
To reduce company photo-copying costs by 5% in the current financial year.	Photocopying costs to be reduced by 5% without reducing quality of supplies and servicing.	28 March.	2% saving to be shown by 31 December and 4% by 28 February.

Chapter 6
Following Up

Following up on the action agreed at appraisal time is a discipline which assists in making the whole process a continuous one. There must be commitment from senior management to allowing appraisers to consider follow-up as much a part of their job as budgeting or health and safety. In a consultation meeting about their appraisal scheme, a group of junior managers in a northern manufacturing company said that they felt that the basic structure of the scheme was very adequate, but the reason that they had requested the meeting, was to question the company's apparent lack of commitment to follow-up. Without it, they felt that their own appraisals had not been worthwhile, and they were not given the time and resources to follow-up on the appraisals of their staff. Fortunately, this group had the sense to address the problem and get something done about it. They had recognised and communicated what a phenomenal waste of time and resources appraisal is without any sort of follow-up attached to it.

Credibility

Following up on appraisal is about credibility — of the appraisal scheme, of the management, of the organisation, and of the individuals who carry out appraisal.

Something must be seen to happen as a result of appraisal. This may be at an organisational level or at an individual level. Either way, it must be understood that the exercise will be totally wasted if, once interviews are over, report forms are filed and forgotten.

The co-ordinating officer has responsibility here in assessing and acting upon the more widespread needs highlighted by the appraisal process. However, the responsibility of individual follow-up stays very firmly with managers. What methods they use to ensure that this is done effectively should merely complement whatever system they would normally use to ensure that things get done. It does not matter how managers organise themselves, (year planners, progress charts, diaries, bring forward systems), as long as every action plan is followed up in a constructive manner, within the time limits agreed.

Individual Feedback

Recognition that something has been achieved is a significant part of following up on action plans. There can be few things more demotivating than putting a great deal of effort into improving performance, only to have such efforts ignored. Not all action plans are going to produce successful outcomes at the first attempt. In fact, it is important to recognise in some cases that it is highly likely that real achievement will only come after a series of attempts have been made to get performance moving in the right direction. Careful planning and staging is necessary in such cases to ensure that the motivation to keep trying is not lost.

Dealing with failure is an element of follow-up which cannot be overlooked. Realistically, employees do not fail on the day that they were due to complete an item of their action plan. Impending failure becomes apparent long before that stage and if the monitoring and support from the manager is adequate, it will be picked up and dealt with before it has to be openly declared. Investigating reasons, replanning and restructuring can head off disaster, the repercussions of which can be devastating, since the focus of action planning is intended to be motivation by achievement.

Appraising Appraisers

Reviewing managers need to consider the departments and managers they are responsible for as a part of their appraisal follow-up. Picking up on trends which emerge demonstrates that senior managers take the appraisal process seriously and are prepared to take action as a result of it.

Similarly, reviewing managers need to consider their managers as appraisers, ensuring that they are fair, consistent and conscientious in carrying out their appraisal duties. More pertinently, if they are not, then something should be done about it so that mistakes are not perpetuated. Part of this action, would be to get managers to consider their own talents as appraisers and agree with them how their skills could be improved.

Appraising Appraisal

A worthwhile appraisal system will have built into it a mechanism whereby feedback about the scheme itself can be collated and acted upon. This feedback should be encouraged from all levels of staff and put together via analysis or consultation meetings, by the co-ordinating officer. As organisations develop, their systems must develop to keep pace with changing priorities and needs.

Often, all that is needed is some fine tuning, particularly if the appraisal scheme is new. One "run" is rarely enough to make an objective decision about a new scheme, simply because people have to get used to the demands it makes of them. However, ignoring elements which are obviously not working effectively is going to have an adverse effect on the general impact of the scheme on its users.

This fifth step in carrying out effective performance appraisal serves to bring this dissertation full circle. The test of effective appraisal is whether or not it meets the objectives which were set for it in the first place. Given that these objectives were relevant and realistic, then the answer should be a resounding "Yes!". Any doubts at all must be considered carefully and addressed competently to ensure the continued validity of performance appraisal in the organisation.

Chapter 7
Conclusion

Summary of Key Points

Writing or Revising Job Descriptions

(a) The first step in carrying out performance appraisal effectively is to write or revise job descriptions and ensure that staff are able to use them.

(b) The format and style of job descriptions will vary according to different organisations' needs. The style in use should be reviewed periodically to ensure its continued relevance.

(c) Job descriptions are also useful in selection procedures, analysing training requirements, supporting disciplinary procedures, reviewing organisational structure, grading jobs and making the scope of the job holder's authority clear.

(d) Job descriptions should be kept up to date and appraisal time is a useful opportunity to involve employees in this exercise.

(e) Involving job holders in compiling or revising job descriptions will give clearer insight into the detail of the job and how it is viewed by those who have to carry it out.

(f) Job descriptions should have a clear structure which includes the overall objective of the job and details of duties, either listed or broken down into key areas. There should be an emphasis on using clear and unambiguous terms to describe duties.

(g) However much detail the chosen format goes into, a balance should be found between making the job description so vague that it is not helpful and so detailed that it is complicated and inhibiting.

(h) There is a requirement for consistency in the format of job description chosen across an organisation, although it may be desirable to use a less prescriptive style at more senior levels.

(i) Flexibility in the use of job descriptions should be facilitated by the judicious use of an "any other reasonable task ..." section.

(j) The setting of standards is important if there is to be any assessment of performance.

(k) Standards must be clear, achievable and expressed in measurable terms.

(l) Setting standards has a further practical use where minimum standards of safety, security, budgeting, authority, frequency, timing, quantity and quality should be stated.

(m) Care should be taken not to approach the setting of standards in a way which would not be consistent with an organisation's normal management style.

(n) It is easy to quantify measurable standards for some jobs, whilst others have less tangible features. Where this is the case, it is helpful to describe these aspects in terms of the actions required to carry them out.

(o) Standards of performance should be communicated adequately to job holders. The job description can fulfil this function by cross-referencing to various procedures and guidelines, or by describing standards alongside the various duties of the job.

(p) Staff should always have full access to their job descriptions and standards of performance and be encouraged to refer to them bearing in mind that this forms the first of the steps leading to effective performance.

Preparing for the Appraisal Meeting

(a) A good performance appraisal interview is as much a preparation skill as a communication skill.

(b) Appraisees should be given 10–14 days' warning that their appraisal interview is due. Part of the reminder could be a "Preparation for appraisal" form which may be returned voluntarily before the interview date to assist the manager's preparation.

(c) Cover should be arranged so that the interview is not rushed because of operational needs.

(d) The appraisal interview should always be carried out in a private and relaxed environment in which both parties are physically and psychologically comfortable.

(e) It is not possible to estimate how long an appraisal meeting might take, so when scheduling interviews managers should allow at least the whole morning or whole afternoon. Two a day is as much as most managers could effectively cope with.

(f) By far the largest task in preparing for appraisal is the manager's consideration of the whole review period.

(g) Considering how appraisees have matched up to the standards stated in their job descriptions or to the objectives which have been agreed with them is a good starting point for preparation. Care must be taken to focus on the whole review period, not just recent events.

(h) It is essential to establish the facts about both good and bad performance by the use of examples.

(i) Considering the possible reasons for good performance can give a clearer insight into an employee's particular talents, potential and ambitions. However, beware of the "halo" effect.

(j) Only by uncovering the reasons for poor performance can action be planned to ensure standards will improve. In this case, beware of the "horns" effect.

(k) Feedback from the right people is a vital part of preparing for appraisal, although the appraising manager must be satisfied about the validity and objectivity of information received.

(l) Certain items of documentation such as job descriptions, previous appraisals, personal files and examples need to be brought together in preparing for appraisal. The appraisal report form should *not* be completed in advance lest the outcome of the appraisal meeting is seen to be a foregone conclusion.

(m) An interview plan is essential to ensure that everything is fully discussed at the appraisal meeting. There are various methods of constructing an appraisal agenda, the most effective possibly being to let the appraisee decide the batting order. The manager's agenda then simply forms a check-list of items to be covered.

Conducting Appraisal Interviews

(a) The objective of an appraisal interview is to research and to plan ahead for mutual gain.

(b) The "joint approach" should be used in appraisal interviewing, based on the idea that confrontation and imposition are not the best ways to get commitment from appraisees to making improvements. Ideally, appraisees' awareness is developed and agreement is gained for future action.

(c) Appraisers should spend some time at the beginning of interviews in creating the right atmosphere, building rapport and setting out the parameters and structure of the meeting.

(d) Open questions should be used to get appraisees talking, but the skilful use of all types of question will ensure a balanced interview.

(e) Appraisers should demonstrate listening skills by various physical indicators such as eye contact. However, the proof of real listening is in how questions are linked and how accurate notes appear to have been when summaries are made from them.

(f) Appraisers need to keep careful control of interviews by coping with talkative people and getting the less talkative to open up. They also need to ensure that the meeting does not drift into other areas, that employees voice their honest opinions and that confrontation does not develop beyond constructive bounds.

(g) Summaries made throughout the appraisal interview are useful in structuring the meeting and in checking understanding. A final summary is necessary to ensure that the appraisal interview has reached its objectives and can be satisfactorily concluded.

(h) The most important summary takes place at a later meeting when the appraisal report has been written and is ready to be signed as an accurate record of the discussion.

Agreeing Action Plans

(a) The action which will result from an appraisal interview will be to bring weaker areas up to standard, to develop satisfactory or stronger areas and to give appraisees goals to work towards in the following months.

(b) Action plans need to be:

(i)   agreed
(ii)   distributed carefully in relation to job content
(iii) achievable, having considered likely external influences
(iv)   clear in intent
(v)   relevant
(vi)   appropriate
(vii) related to organisational as well as appraisees' needs
(viii) specifically outlined, with clear standards, controls, time frames and limits of authority
(ix)   carefully spaced out and monitored
(x)   varied in the degree of challenge offered.

Follow-up

(a) Following up action plans agreed at appraisal assists in keeping the process a continuous one. Follow-up is important to maintain the credibility of the appraisal scheme, the management of the organisation and the individuals who carry out appraisal.

(b) Something must be seen to happen as a result of appraisal, both at an organisational and an individual level.

(c) The responsibility for individual follow-up rests firmly with managers, who should incorporate their efforts to maintain the momentum of appraisal into their normal priorities.

(d) Individuals must be given recognition and feedback about their progress in carrying out action plans.

(e) Potential failure should be picked up and dealt with before it causes serious demotivation.

(f) Senior managers should review the departments and managers they are responsible for to pick up and act on trends, and to consider the abilities of their managers as appraisers.

(g) Feedback about the appraisal scheme from all levels of staff should be co-ordinated, so that it can be considered in the light of making any necessary changes to keep the scheme as effective as possible.

(h) The test of effectiveness should be whether or not appraisal has met its stated objectives. The answer to this question should be yes, but if it is not, then concerns must be competently addressed to ensure the continued validity of performance appraisal in the organisation.

Check-list for Managing Performance Appraisal

Should elements of this text assist in the initiative to develop and manage a performance appraisal scheme, the following summary has been distilled from the main practical points to form a check-list for managers involved in the process.

(a) Is the term "performance appraisal" fully understood to mean a regular meeting between managers and their staff to agree present and future *performance* issues? Is it also understood that appraisal is a continuous responsibility and that the appraisal meeting represents a "landmark" in this process?

(b) Have objectives for the scheme been considered and are they consistent with organisational aims?

(c) Does the scheme complement the management style and practices which are the norm in the organisation?

(d) Has any relationship with reward been carefully thought out?

(e) Have potential problem areas been considered?

(f) Is there commitment from the very top of the organisation?

(g) How are "users" going to be communicated with to ensure ownership, during the design phase?

(h) Who is going to guide matters so that the most appropriate scheme will emerge from the consultation and design stage?

(i) Will appraisees be able to identify readily with the stated objectives of the scheme and see the relevance of them?

(j) Has the design of the performance appraisal scheme been considered with specific reference to enabling it to meet its objectives?

(k) Is the scheme going to be consistently and fairly applied throughout the organisation? How and by whom is this to be ensured?

(l) Is the scheme going to be an open one which emphasises participation in reaching agreement about matters of performance, so that the way ahead can be established to maximise effectiveness?

(m) Will associated paperwork be relevant and "user friendly"?

(n) Will the scheme be confidential? How is feedback going to be handled?

(o) Will it reflect an equal opportunities policy in implementation?

(p) How will the implementation of the scheme be communicated?

(q) Will training for both appraisers and appraisees be planned?

(r) Has the use of job descriptions in relation to the scheme been considered? How complete is employees' understanding of their jobs and the standards required?

(s) Will appraisers and appraisees be made aware of the vital importance of sound preparation in the process of carrying out effective performance appraisal?

(t) Will interviews be conducted with a clear emphasis on a joint approach, to ensure that commitment will be gained to make lasting improvements?

(u) Will interviews be structured to agree relevant and appropriate development plans to maximise future performance standards?

(v) How will conscientious follow-up be facilitated? This applies not only to following up on appraisees' action plans, but also to how well appraisals have been carried out, and how the design and implementation of the scheme have fared in relation to assisting it to meet its objectives.

Index

ACAS code of practice,
  disciplinary procedures, 12
Action plans,
  characteristics, 115–18
  essential principles, 118–19,
    128–9
  example, 119–20
  timing, 118
Administration, 67–8
Appeals procedure, 67
Appearance, 12
Appraisal forms, 34, 57–62, 77,
    112–13
  examples, 49, 50, 61–4
  preparation forms, 56–7
    example, 59–60
  signature, 113
  structure and content, 57–8
Appraisal interview see interview
Appraisee,
  notice of interview, 93, 126
  preparing for interview, 93–4,
    126–7

Appraising appraisal, 123
Appraising appraisers, 122–3
Apprehension, reducing, 108
Assessment of performance, 96–8
  compared with appraising, 9, 33

Behaviour, 11, 33, 76
Benefits of performance appraisal,
    26

Check-list, 131–2
Closed question, 105, 108
Closed scheme, 48, 55, 66, 76
Commission for Racial Equality,
    66
Communication, 10, 18–19, 34,
    42, 45–6, 69–70, 132
  summary of key points, 78–9
Computerised personnel records,
    66, 78
Conduct see Behaviour
Confidentiality, 65, 77, 132
Consulting users, 42, 43–4

summary of key points, 76
Continuous appraisal, benefits, 12
Copies, 58

Data Protection Act 1984, 66, 78
Definition of performance
    appraisal, 9
Designing performance appraisal
    scheme, 47–63, 132
    appraisal forms *see* Appraisal
        forms
    aspects to discuss, 49–50
    examples, 49, 50
    frequency, 54, 77
    management led or joint, 48–9,
        76
    narrative form of assessment,
        50, 53, 77
    open or closed, 48, 76
    rating form of assessment, 49,
        51–3, 77
    staff included, 47–8, 76
    summary of key points, 76–7
    timing, 54–5
Developing performance appraisal
    scheme, agenda example,
        43–4
Disciplinary issues, 12–13, 33, 67,
    78
Discrimination, evidence of, 66
Documentation, collecting
    together, 99–100, 127

Employees,
    communication with *see*
        Communication with users
    labour-intensive production,
        30–1
Equal opportunities, 66, 78, 132

Evaluating performance, 11
Eye contact, 109, 128

Face-to-face meetings, 69, 78
Fairness, ensuring, 65
Feedback,
    co-ordinating, 66
    from appraisal, 24, 77–8
    from users, 70, 129
    individual, 122
Following up on action agreed,
    121–3, 132
    credibility, 121–2, 129
    responsibility of manager, 122,
        129
    summary of key points, 129
Frequency, 54, 77
Future, considerations for, 14–15,
    34

Hypothetical question, 106, 108

Interview,
    agenda, 100–101, 127
    manager's review, 95–101
    notice of interview to appraisee,
        93, 126
    objective, 103, 128
    preparation, 93–101
        appraisee, 93–4
        practical, 94–5, 127
        summary of key points,
            126–7
    privacy, 94, 127
    room layout, 95
    timing, 95
Interviewing skills,
    creating rapport, 107–8, 128
    disagreement, 111–12

drifting into other types of
  interview, 110
getting people to open up,
  109–10
joint approach, 103–7, 128, 132
keeping control, 109–112
listening skills, 109,128
opening the interview, 107–8
over-compliance, 110–11
questioning, 108–9
summaries, 112–13, 128
talkative appraisee, 109
Introducing appraisal scheme, 1

Job content, 25
Job descriptions, 28, 29, 35, 36, 98
  access to, 91–2, 126
  communicating standards, 90–1
  detail required, 87–8, 125–6
  items included, 86
  summary of key points, 125–6
  terminology, 86
  uses, 85, 132
  validity, 56–7
  writing, 85–8
Joint approach, 48, 103–7, 128,
  132
  description, 76, 103–4
  sample extract, 104–7

Labour turnover see Staff retention
Line managers, responsibilities, 2
Listening skills, 109

Management,
  commitment, 31
  consultation with others, 99
  responsibilities, 2, 122, 129
  review, 95–101
  style, 17–18, 34, 131

Management-led appraisal
  scheme, 48, 76
Manpower planning, 24
Meaning of performance appraisal,
  9–15, 131
  summary of key points, 33–4
Monitoring, 66
Motivation, 19–20, 34–5
Motivators, 19

Narrative form of assessment,
  53, 77
  example, 50
Negative attitudes, 1–2, 29, 36

Objectives, 17–26, 131
  communicating to employees,
    45–6, 76
  examples, 18, 45–6
  formulating, 45–6, 76
    summary of key points, 76
  improving communications,
    18–19, 34
    summary of key points, 34–6
One-to-one basis of appraisal, 9,
  34
Open question, 104, 105, 106,
  108, 109, 128
  hypothetical, 106
Open scheme, 48, 55, 66, 76, 132

Paperwork, 28–9, 67, 78, 132
Participative style of management,
  1
Pay, relating to performance,
  20–2, 35
Performance,
  good, reasons for, 96–7, 127
  poor, reasons for, 96, 97–8, 127
Personality, 13–14, 33–4, 66, 76

Preparation forms, 56–7, 127
  example, 59–60
Probing closed question, 105
Problems of performance
  appraisal,
  ability, 28
  attitudes, 1–2, 29, 36
  job descriptions, 28, 29, 36
  management commitment, 31
  operating structure, 29–31, 36
  paperwork, 28–9
  summary of key points, 36
  time, 27
Procedural aspects,
  guidelines for managers,
  example, 67–8
  summary of key points, 77–8
Project workers, 30
Promotion, 22, 35

Question types, 104–7
Questioning statement, 104

Race Relations Act 1976, 66
Rapport, creating, 107–8
Rating form of assessment, 51–3,
  77
  example, 49
Rebound question, 105, 108, 109
Record of appraisal, 14, 25–6
Regularity, 10
Results achieved, measurement of
  performance, 11, 33
Review by next management level,
  65
Revising appraisal scheme, 1
Reward, 20–2
Role play, 72

Salary awards, using appraisal, 58
Self-assessment, 56, 94
Sex Discrimination Act 1975, 66
Shared scheme of appraisal, 49, 76
Signature, 58
Silence, use in interview, 105,
  108, 109
Specific question, 105, 106, 108
Staff handbook, 70
Staff retention, 26, 35
Standards of performance, 23,
  88–91
  communicating, 90–1
  need for, 88
  negative measurements, 91
  setting, 88–90, 126
Statement, 104, 105, 106
Summaries, during interview, 77,
  112–13

Talkative appraisee, 109
Talking, ratio of, 108
Time–keeping, 12
Timing, 54–5
Training,
  appraisees, 73, 132
  appraisers, 70–2, 78–9, 132
  summary of key points, 78–9
Training and development needs,
  23–4, 35

Workforce, scattered, 29–30